Celebrating Quiet Leaders: Uplifting Stories of Introverted Leaders Who Changed History

Prasenjeet Kumar

Published by Prasen Publishers LLP, 2015.

CELEBRATING QUIET LEADERS: UPLIFTING STORIES OF INTROVERTED LEADERS WHO CHANGED HISTORY

First edition. September 23, 2015.

Copyright © 2015 Prasenjeet Kumar.

ISBN: 978-8197187988

Written by Prasenjeet Kumar.

Table of Contents

Introduction 1

Chapter 1: A shy, awkward lad becomes the greatest Military Leader in English History...... 6

Chapter 2: Be your own beacon, prescribe no Holy Book, terrorise no one and yet have a billion followers 17

Chapter 3: The Grey Wolf who took on the Religious Clergy and forged a Modern Nation 29

Chapter 4: The Courageous Lion 38

Chapter 5: Was Jesus an introvert? 45

Chapter 6: Leading From Behind to Rescue a Pariah Nation 51

Chapter 7: The Teacher who stopped Alexander the Great and Knitted a Formidable Empire 60

Chapter 8: The Quiet Leader who declined to be King.. 71

Chapter 9: The Quiet Mr. Light Who Took on a Superpower and Won 79

Chapter 10: The Quiet Angel of Crimea...... 89

Chapter 11: A Living god is exiled but the world still bows before him 96

Chapter 12: Confucius in the 21st Century...... 107

The End 119

Books by Prasenjeet Kumar in the Quiet Phoenix Series...... 121

Acknowledgment 124

Disclaimer 125

Connect With The Author 126

About The Author...... 127

Introduction

Dear Quiet friend,

I hope the title of this book would have intrigued you enough to cajole you to preview it a bit.

The theme of this book is if introverts can really lead? And if yes, can they just lead, as any imbecile hereditary heir to the throne is expected to, or provide legendary leadership?

We do live in a society where it is drilled into our heads that in order to successfully lead you must act assertively, boldly and be willing to take the centre stage. In the process, not only do you have to be fine with such 'qualities' as arrogance and over-confidence but in some circumstances it is even considered desirable to carefully cultivate such traits.

If you are quiet and shy, you will be asked to overcome your "shyness" or "introversion". Or forget your dreams of leading anyone.

"Awaken your extroverted self", they tell you.

Let me clear the misconception right away. Introverts cannot only lead but make outstanding leaders.

For my research, I had to plod through quite a few books and articles on introverts who History recognises as successful leaders. And I was surprised with what I found.

I discovered that introverts were not only successful as leaders but ultra-successful! And most of them are so extremely well-known that you will be surprised.

More importantly, they succeeded not because they could overcome their introversion, BUT because of their introversion.

Introverts have been successful in supposedly all extroverted fields of leadership be it military, politics, academics, or religion. Some led their troops into the battlefield (violently) while others led quietly, non-violently or passively.

So what has made these introverts so successful?

Introverts are gifted with some natural strengths which if utilised well can turn any quiet person into a successful leader. First among these is a rich imagination. We speak less but think a lot. The outside world does not know what we are thinking. But the same thought process can lead to a vision or a dream.

Every successful introverted leader in the 'stories' narrated in this book had a rich vision. He or she dreamt of seeing her people free or envisaged a nation that safeguarded the health and happiness of its people.

Next, these leaders took small but concrete steps to set up institutions that delivered results and carried forward their vision even hundreds of years after they were gone.

Third, introverts have an analytical mind and are cautious by nature. You may think that a cautious person may not excel in military matters where throwing yourself straight into the battlefield is considered valour. But you may be amazed to know that some of the greatest military generals in history were defensive by nature. They were able to pull out some amazing victories only because they took the time to think, plan and act decisively. They carefully studied the terrain, tactics and the weaknesses of their enemies. And they didn't lead by making grandiose speeches but by setting an example.

Which takes me to the fourth point. Introverts by nature do not like to be the centre of attention. Then how can they make excellent leaders? Remember the old saying *"Action speaks louder than words."* We live in a world where our so-called leaders promise too many things (eloquently) but deliver on none. For introverts, it is easier to act than to say. This is a strength NOT a weakness. And this is what makes people believe in your integrity and character.

In many of the stories to come, you will read about how shy people kept sitting when they were asked to stand and then driven by an inner voice picked up a broom and started sweeping the floor that led to the greatest revolutions of all times. These were all simple acts. There was no grandiose, no earth-shaking act of bravery and yet the outcome took quite a few breaths away.

As a leader, you are expected to make speeches. But if you don't like making speeches, how on earth can you then lead a revolution?

Don't worry. I find that when introverted leaders spoke, they spoke out of conviction. Their speeches touched a chord because it came straight from their hearts. As an introverted leader, it is easier to speak when your passions are aroused.

You may be shy in real life and troubled by bullies but when you see someone chopping a tree or shooting at a bird your passions are aroused. You are no longer shy or afraid to confront. You may even risk your life by standing up to protect a tree or to save a bird's life. And you are not alone.

Your fellow quiet leaders that you are about to meet in the coming pages had all their passions aroused at some point. Though reserved by nature, our quiet leaders stood up to take cudgels and when they did that, they did so brilliantly.

And finally a word about religion. You may think that most prominent religious leaders were extroverts who carried God's message eloquently. But let me surprise you once again: they were most likely introverts who just felt a close connection with God or their "inner selves".

This book contains stories about military, political, academic and religious leaders but the same principles can be applied to any business set up.

So, ladies and gentlemen, be prepared to immerse yourselves into tales of courage and valour shown by quiet, shy and sensitive men and women from ALL AROUND THE WORLD. You will read how these quiet leaders faced the biggest challenges and threats of their lives and how they rose from the ashes like the legendary Phoenix bird BUT quietly.

Like a 'Quiet Phoenix', as I call this series of books.

Most of these leaders are well-known. Therefore, in order to keep the mystery going, I have tried to hide their true identities just a little.

Warning: Don't be surprised if you find that these leaders sound quite like you.

And even if you are an extrovert, I am sure you will learn a lot about leadership in general.

I wish you a happy reading!

Sincerely yours,

Prasenjeet

Chapter 1: A shy, awkward lad becomes the greatest Military Leader in English History

On 7th February 1847, Angela Burdett-Coutts, one of the richest women in the world, proposed to Arthur. That shouldn't have created any ripples in the then English Society except that Arthur then was seventy-eight and Angela was thirty-three.

Despite the age difference, there was no doubt that Arthur was a worthy suitor. He was a much decorated military man, rising to the post of the Commander-in-Chief of the British Army. He had been an ambassador, a parliamentarian and even the Prime Minister of England for a short period.

By all accounts, Arthur had developed a close relationship with Angela. At first this involved advising her on business matters. But later, as Edna Healey, the author of "Lady Unknown: The Life of Angela Burdett-Coutts" (1978), asserts: "The tone of his letters, the winding staircase to his private rooms, the intertwined locks of hair show how close it was."

Also this was not the usual celebrity-fan infatuation. Feelings were being reciprocated equally. It was whispered that, when they were apart, Arthur wrote to Angela daily, sometimes twice a day. It has been estimated that during the time they knew each other Arthur sent Miss Burdett-Coutts over 800 letters! They often sent each other the "product of their walks", a flower, a delicate leaf, a fragrant herb.

This naturally sent tongues wagging. Granville Leveson-Gower recorded disapprovingly that Arthur: "was astonishing the world by a strange intimacy he has struck up with Miss Coutts with whom he passes his life, and all sorts of reports have been rife of his intention to marry her. Such are the lamentable appearances of decay in his vigorous mind, which are more to be regretted because he is in most enviable circumstances, without any political responsibility, yet associated with public affairs, and surrounded with every sort of respect and consideration on every side - at Court, in Parliament, in society, and in the country."

Arthur was a widower with his wife having died of cancer, in 1831, some 16 years back. He had a few dalliances before too. One of his mistresses, Harriette Wilson, even tried to blackmail him by threatening to write about their relationship, to which Arthur famously replied: "publish and be damned."

There was, therefore, no reason why he shouldn't be marrying Ms. Coutts.

Yet Arthur wrote to her a letter the following day:

"My dearest Angela, I have passed every moment of the evening and night since I quitted you in reflecting upon our conversation of yesterday, every word of which I have considered repeatedly. My first duty towards you is that of friend, guardian, and protector. You are young, my dearest! You have before you the prospect of at least twenty years of enjoyment of happiness in life. I entreat you again in this way, not to throw yourself away upon a man old enough to be your grandfather, who, however strong, hearty and healthy at present, must and will certainly in time feel the consequences and infirmities of age... My last days would be embittered by the reflection that your life was uncomfortable and hopeless."

What kind of a strange person this Arthur was, to who the welfare of the other party overrode his own needs and desires?

For this we shall have to go back a little in History.

Arthur was born in 1769, the same year that Napoleon was born in Corsica. He lost his father, the Earl of Mornington in Dublin, Ireland, at an early age. He was considered a reserved, withdrawn child. "I vow to God I don't know what I shall do with my awkward son Arthur," lamented his mother once.

In 1781, when he was eleven years old, Arthur was sent to Eton, one of the most elitist of schools in 18th century England. The school prided itself for giving England its Lords, Knights and Barons. However, all hopes were dashed when the boy showed no signs of improvement.

Arthur remained "an unsociable and occasionally aggressive schoolboy who made little effort to learn." His only interest seemed to be in playing the violin. The boy was without any friends and showed little to no talent for doing anything. Worse, the boy underperformed in his studies. He came fifty-fourth out of seventy nine in his school.

Arthur's mother was convinced that her ugly son was "fit food for powder, and nothing more." She had, therefore, Arthur removed from Eton in the summer of 1784 and packed off to Brussels to learn French. In January 1786, he was sent to the Academy of Equitation at Angers, France.

France in the late 1700s was considered the place where boys were turned into "real men," whatever that meant. At

Angers, Arthur learnt the art of fencing, horsemanship and fortification. Within a year, a new Arthur was born: a man with remarkable self-assurance and confidence.

On Christmas Day, 1787, Arthur became a lieutenant in an English infantry regiment. He was still a shy, introverted man, in whom no one saw anything attractive.

One night at a large ball, Arthur was unable to find a dancing partner. So he simply sat down near the band to enjoy music while others were happily dancing with their partners. After the ball was over, everyone left with their partners in a cheerful mood. Arthur had to leave with the fiddlers!

When Arthur was twenty-one, he was on account of his lineage given a seat in the Irish Parliament.

"Who is that young man in scarlet uniform with large epaulettes?" once commented a visitor to the Irish House of Commons.

"That is Arthur," replied one of Arthur's colleagues.

"I suppose he never speaks," remarked the visitor.

"You are wrong," said the colleague, "he does speak. And when he does, it is always to the point."

After picking up the rank of major in 1793, Arthur gathered courage to propose to Lady Catherine Sarah Dorothea Pakenham, sister of Thomas Packenham, 2nd Duke of Longford. The offer was refused by her brother on the grounds that Arthur lacked the prospect of being able to support her properly.

Arthur's response to this rejection was violent. He set fire to his violin and decided to focus on active military service.

Arthur decided to get the rank of Lieutenant Colonel. In those days, buying ranks within the military was common in

England and Arthur with some support from his brother was able to "buy his promotion".

The English Army then used to be quite disorganised. Criminals were recruited into the army as a punishment. Army service was seen as "an alternative to exile, prison or death". Even those who joined voluntarily were often unemployable in civilian life. The soldiers were either unskilled or alcoholic or both. There was hardly any military training. They were literally the "scum of the earth".

Time had come for Lieutenant Colonel Arthur to use his gifted strengths of introversion to reform the British Army which seemed like an impossible task. As an introvert, Arthur was naturally endowed with the powers of intuition. He instinctively seemed to know which soldier was best for which task and at what time. He appointed his friend Beresford to command the Portuguese troops (who were allies of the British against the French) because he was an intelligent and strong-willed drillmaster. This was one of Arthur's best appointments. The soldiers who were poorly trained were used only for defence.

Next Arthur made following orders mandatory in the army. In those days, following orders was less important than displaying valour in the battlefield. Arthur believed in strict discipline. So he enforced a code whereby soldiers were frequently punished for defiance.

At the same time, he rewarded disciplined soldiers by promoting them. Arthur also took great care of his men by ensuring that they were provided with regular pay, adequate food, clothing, shoes and bedding.

Being painfully shy, Arthur never led by giving any grand speeches. In fact, as he admitted readily, he was mortally scared of being booed if he tried to address them!

"How did he then motivate his men?" is a question that naturally comes to mind.

Unlike his other rank conscience colleagues, who only mixed with officers of their rank and status, Arthur freely mingled even with such officers who were junior to him, especially during meal times. As a good introvert, he was genuinely good at one-on-one conversations. He often rode with his men and engaged in friendly banter. This was one of the reasons that Arthur was affectionately referred to as the "Peer" by his colleagues.

In 1796, Arthur's Regiment was posted to India. His brother, Richard as the then-Governor-General of India, ordered the invasion of the Southern State of Mysore on the suspicion that its ruler Tipu Sultan was getting too close to the French. Arthur captured Mysore on the 4th of May, 1799 and Tipu was slain on the battlefield.

In 1803, he was ordered to march against one of the Maratha Rajas who was threatening the English frontiers. Arthur took his troops 120 miles and found a 50,000 strong Maratha army with 128 guns, as opposed to his 7000 men and 17 guns, facing him. Nobody would have expected the British to win this battle.

Arthur's natural introverted ability of 'attention to detail' immediately came in handy. Arthur was looking for a way to fight the Marathas on favourable grounds and in the process spotted two villages on either side of the river. The local guides argued that it was impossible to cross the river; the banks were steep and rocky, and there was no ford. Arthur overruled them and took the risk to attack. He led his Indian troops across the river, outflanked his opponents and defeated them at the battle of Assaye.

As Norman Gash narrates:

"His force, reduced by his questionable decision to send Colonel Stevenson's Hyderabad contingent round by a different route, numbered only 7000. His men had already marched 20 miles that day and retreat would have been almost as hazardous as an advance. He took the bolder course. Guessing correctly that there must be a ford between two villages on opposite sides of the river, he crossed below the left flank of the Maratha position and placed his force in a narrow angle between the Kaitna and a tributary river, the Juah: a position which shortened his front and protected his flanks, but would have been a death-trap had he been beaten. The Marathas, under their French officers, skilfully changed front to meet him, and a desperate battle followed before victory was assured. (Arthur's) right flank advanced too far and came under heavy artillery fire near Assaye village. Of approximately 5000 men who crossed the Kaitna over a third became casualties, a disproportionate number being among the British troops. (Arthur) contributed by his personal example to the result. In the thick of the fighting throughout, he had one horse killed under him and another wounded."

It was a great decision. It was also Arthur's first great battle. Arthur himself was in the thick of the action the whole time, giving his orders as coolly as an experienced veteran. His horse was shot under him, but he mounted another and fought on. By evening the enemy was in full retreat. Arthur had crushed the rebellion, and secured to England her dominions.

For this, he received the thanks of the Parliament and a sword of honour from Calcutta. He was also made a knight—a great honour in those days, when there were only twenty-four knights.

Arthur now was primed for his most challenging moment. In 1815, Arthur led his troops against the seemingly unstoppable Napoleon in the Battle of Waterloo. Using his intuitive strength, Arthur personally selected the positions of each infantry brigade and made decisions to the lowest level possible.

To avoid casualties from Napoleon's artillery, Arthur moved his troops on the reverse slope of the battlefield. This slope worked as a shield for his soldiers from canon fire. The tactics surprised the French because they couldn't see Arthur's troops and thought they had run away!

But when the French Cavalry charged and crossed the point where Arthur was keeping his troops hidden, the British just got up and slaughtered the surprised French. This way Arthur was able to repeatedly crush French columns. At the end of the day, Napoleon was routed. It was often said that the French came on in the old style and were driven off in the old style.

I am indeed talking about the famous Arthur Wellesley, the first Duke of Wellington who proved to be one of the greatest Military Generals in English History. His superior judgement of terrain, tactics and men made him defeat opponents who like Napoleon were far more powerful and flamboyant than him.

Of course, Arthur Wellesley was also an introvert who displayed the same great strengths that most introverted leaders employ. He led by example and exposed himself to the same dangers that his soldiers were exposed to. He was hit twice by bullets and had the horse he was riding killed under him.

His style was remarkably different from other military leaders of the time (like Napoleon or that Maratha king) who gave only orders and watched the battle from a distance. On top of that, Arthur's amazing ability to understand terrain made him a very successful General.

Like most introverts, Arthur was averse to risk taking. He never sacrificed his troops for a quick victory and was quite saddened by war. In fact he has been accused by Historians of being overly cautious and defensive. This was unlike Napoleon who never felt remorse in inflicting catastrophes and getting millions killed in the process. For Napoleon, his troops were completely expendable.

Arthur Wellesley's tactics and moves are still taught in military schools the world over. Like most introverts, he had a very well developed sense of intuition. He knew which tasks precisely suited whom and so he could almost always choose the right person. As a result he was able to transform the British army from a group of bandits to the most disciplined and sophisticated army in the world.

Different people had different opinions about his personality. According to his hostess, Mrs. Granville, he was *"the most unpretentious, perfectly natural and amiable person"* she had ever met.

In Mrs. Arbuthnot's eyes, he was *"the pleasantest person possible in a house, so simple and so easily amused and pleased....It is impossible to know him well without loving him. He is so kind to everybody, so affectionate and so good-natured, and I must say I never did know any man so universally beloved."*

However, for the British Historian Christopher Duffy, Arthur Wellesley *"had this fundamental coldness in his heart. He would weep when he met casualties, but basically he was a cold hearted bastard...(who was) largely responsible for what became the image of a type of English gentleman: reserved, aloof, cold, soberly dressed..."*

Arthur was the Prime Minister of England for a short period. But his dread of democracy, turning into a rule by the mob, made him not so successful in politics. The disdain for the opinion of men, as opposed to the command of an experienced General, is a common trait among military men that Arthur too carried from his days of discipline in the army.

Wellesley remained a bit touchy about his Irish origins. When an enthusiastic Celt once commended him as a famous Irishman, he replied tartly, "A man can be born in a stable, and yet not be an animal."

-This British politician, Prime Minster and Commander-in-Chief was so shy that he rarely spoke even to his servants. He would rather write his orders to them on a note pad, which he often left on his dressing table!

Arthur Wellesley, the Duke of Wellington died at Walmer Castle on 14th September, 1852 and was buried at St Paul's Cathedral. Norman Gash writes that "the occasion for probably the most ornate and spectacular funeral ever seen in England, the procession from Horse Guards via Constitution Hill to St Paul's being witnessed, it was estimated, by a million and a half people."

In his honour, the Wellington Arch still stands in London's Hyde Park. Arthur also gave his name to the humble Wellington boot.

"When my journal appears, many statues must come down."
-Arthur Wellesley, the Duke of Wellington

Chapter 2: Be your own beacon, prescribe no Holy Book, terrorise no one and yet have a billion followers

In the 6th Century B.C., in the forests of Koshala (near the holy city of Ayodhya in India), there lived a fearsome brigand who was called Angulimaal. The thug used to waylay and brutally kill anyone who took the forest routes for whatever purpose. Then in a disgusting and macabre act, the thug used to severe the thumb (anguli) of his victim and wear it as a trophy around his neck in the shape of a garland (mala). By and by, his garland had accumulated 999 thumbs which indicated that he had killed 999 people so far. His publicly stated goal was to collect 1,000 human thumbs. That was why he was called Angulimaal which literally means a finger-garland.

Prasenjeet, the then King of Koshala had sent his armies many a times to catch Angulimaal dead or alive but didn't succeed. The King then heard of a really erudite monk visiting his kingdom and thought of seeking his advice. The serene monk assured Prasenjeet that he will do his best to find Angulimaal.

True to his word, the monk ventured out unarmed in the forests the next day. It was not long before Angulimaal noticed the wandering monk and thought it to be a good idea to kill him and to fulfil his vow of collecting 1,000 thumbs. So he stealthily set out after the monk with his knife raised. But the monk taking long strides kept moving ahead of him. When the panting Angulimaal could not catch up, he shouted asking the monk to stop. The monk paused, turned back and then looking at Angulimaal straight in his eyes, smiled.

Angulimaal was taken off-guard to see the monk's serene and radiant face. Surprised, he couldn't help asking:

"Who are you, O monk and why are you smiling? I have always seen terror on the faces of people when they see me. I have heard them screaming and begging for mercy. How can you be so calm?" demanded Angulimaal.

"Oh Ahimsak (the non-violent one), I have stopped but when are you going to stop?" said the monk rather mysteriously.

"Why do you refer to me as the non-violent one when I have killed 999 human beings? My name is Angulimaal or the man who wears a garland of human fingers, don't you know?" asked the incredulous brigand.

"You have goodness and peace within you. That is why I call you the non-violent one," replied the monk.

This left Angulimaal even more puzzled.

"No, I am evil. This is what everyone agrees about me. I am a bad person. I kill human beings. How can I be good?" argued Angulimaal.

"But you still have got goodness left in your heart. Understand your true nature," insisted the monk.

"That's strange. People call me a thug, dacoit, mass murderer, evil, son of a demon, etc., etc. but you persist in calling me good, the non-violent one," wondered Angulimaal aloud.

It was then that the life of Angulimaal suddenly flashed before his eyes. As a student, he was intelligent, obedient and in fact so bright that his teachers adored him and the other pupils were jealous of him. So some of his classmates thought of playing a prank and told the teacher that Ahimsak, as Angulimal was then called, was having an illegitimate relationship with the teacher's wife. At first the teacher did not believe them but then the story was repeated so many times through so many different sources that the teacher got sick of it all. So one day, the furious teacher asked Ahimsak to just leave the school.

When Ahimsak's father learned of the 'reason' that had led to his son's expulsion, he too lost his temper and asked his son to leave the house. When Ahimsak was walking dejectedly on the streets, some people pointed fingers at him for committing the most grievous sin of sleeping with his guru's wife. Some even started throwing stones at poor Ahimsak. Bruised and bloodied Ahimsak swore to take revenge on the entire humanity by taking a vow to cut and collect 1,000 human thumbs, fingers that were raised in accusation against him.

As he recalled his entire life, tears started rolling down Angulimaal's cheek. He fell on his knees before the serene monk and asked for forgiveness.

"Is it too late to embrace goodness, the noble monk?" asked Angulimaal.

"No, it is never too late," replied the monk.

"Take me with you, the enlightened one. Show me the path of light," begged Angulimaal.

The spies of the King of Koshala reported that Angulimaal was not only located but was now residing with the monk in his camp. Curious, Prasenjeet the King came to look for him, and he saw a man with his head shaved wearing a saffron robe meditating in solitude with his eyes closed. The King could not believe that he was seeing the same dreaded bandit who had once terrorised his kingdom so much.

It is said that Prasenjeet was so impressed that he put the full resources of his kingdom at the disposal of this great monk and in fact became the first royal patron of the enlightened one.

So who was this monk? For this, let's go a little further in history.

The year was 560 B.C. There was jubilation all around Kapilvastu, the small kingdom on the border of India and Nepal because the queen of the Sakya King Shudhodhana had just given birth to a son. Holy men were called to bless the heir to the throne and they named him Siddhartha.

Shudhodhana wanted to make his son the greatest warrior of all times so that he could conquer newer territories and extend the name and fame of the King's empire in all directions. However, when he asked his astrologers to predict his son's future, they were puzzled.

"Would my son be the greatest warrior of all times?" asked the King.

"Your son will definitely become a warrior but he will win the hearts and minds of people through love, compassion and kindness," answered the chief astrologer.

"Would my son fight great battles?" asked the King again.

"Yes, your highness. Your son will fight great battles. But it will be a battle of emotions than a battle of swords," was the intriguing answer of the astrologer.

The King was a little upset. The astrologer was reputed to be infallible. All his predictions used to come true.

And then the astrologer did something which he had never done before.

"I bow in front of this holy soul," said the astrologer to the baby bowing down in reverence.

After the astrologer left, the head priest advised the King to keep the new born away from any kind of suffering, especially disease, old age and death. This was not easy. The city streets had to be cleaned of all the old, diseased and the poor.

So the King ordered that a new town be created especially for them. All the old, diseased and the poor were relocated there. This new town was called the City of Sorrow as it did not have any young or healthy people.

The young prince was given martial training and he was developing into quite a capable swordsman. Siddhartha liked horse-riding too. The only problem was that any blood-letting even during routine exercises used to terribly upset him. For that reason Siddhartha could never be interested into hunting wild animals, which was otherwise considered to be the ultimate act of machismo in those days.

In due course, Siddhartha was married to a beautiful princess Yashodhara. The couple were soon blessed with a son Rahul.

The King was still trying his best to keep the prince ignorant about old age, disease and death behind the palace walls. However, people were growing old or falling sick every day. Shifting them to the City of Sorrow even once a week was a logistical nightmare.

One day, while coming back from his practice grounds, the Prince saw a silver haired man walking with a bent gait.

"What kind of a person is that?" asked the Prince.

"He is old, my Prince. This is what happens to all of us when we age," said the Prince's Charioteer somewhat matter-of-fact.

Another day, the Prince lost his way and wandered into the City of Sorrow by accident. Siddhartha was horrified to see the city full of sick and old people. Then those people surrounded the prince and berated him for keeping them away from their families in their hour of need.

The Prince was deeply disturbed. His mind was swirling with only one question:

"Why do human beings suffer so much and whether there is a way to end suffering?"

Siddhartha had just turned 29 when he decided to bid goodbye to his beautiful wife and sleeping son and to leave the palace in search for the ULTIMATE TRUTH. He shaved off his hair and donned a saffron robe in place of his resplendent royal clothes. He wandered around with other priests and hermits learning their ways but was not satisfied. None of them could answer the Prince's question about the cause of suffering and its cure. Siddhartha read all the Scriptures but they too could not provide him the answers he was seeking.

Then the Prince came across a group of monks who called themselves "Jains". They asked Siddhartha to give up everything including food and water because suffering only could get you to the ULTIMATE TRUTH.

So the Prince survived only by eating a few leaves and nuts and then gave up food and water altogether. After a few days, this ritual made Siddhartha so weak that he collapsed and nearly drowned himself in a nearby pond. He was rescued by a woman who gave him some kheer or sweet rice pudding to eat. The prince regained some energy and realised that an extreme ascetic life could not lead to ultimate happiness. There had to be a MIDDLE PATH between asceticism and self-indulgence.

One day, when he was about 35, Siddhartha decided to sit under a shady Banyan tree and just reflected on whatever he had learnt and observed so far in the last six years. Sacred texts of those days report that the prince thus meditated for a record 49 days. During this period, Siddhartha is said to have debated and conquered all evil forces like greed, lust and anger.

At the end of those 49 days, when he opened his eyes, Siddhartha's face was glowing with infinite wisdom. He was radiating happiness, peace, love and compassion as if he had achieved enlightenment. His colleagues could not help but notice this transformation and in reverence referred to him as "Buddha" or the enlightened one.

With just five followers, who formed the first Buddhist Council, Buddha's fame grew far and wide. Thousands joined his order. It was so easy to understand his definition of the ULTIMATE TRUTH, which is, nothing is permanent. Neither sorrow nor happiness, neither poverty nor wealth—-everything will change. So live in the present. Do good deeds. Be non-violent. If you are born, you will die. So don't be unduly attached to anything, and so on.

Buddha spread his message by actually harnessing the methods and techniques familiar to the introvert, which are of quiet solitude, the exploration of one's inner self, and by talking to people one on one.

Buddha was very fond of telling stories and through his stories he converted people one by one to his ideology of peace and non-violence. And his followers then followed the same technique growing the legion of practising Buddhists to many fold.

A woman came to Buddha one day. Her baby had suddenly died. The woman was distraught and was desperately looking for a 'medicine' that could bring her baby back to life. The local villagers told her about the miraculous powers of the Buddha and so the woman implored Buddha to use all his powers to bring the child alive.

The woman was obviously not amenable to logic. So Buddha promised to help but only on one condition. The woman had to get some mustard seeds from a household that was untouched by death.

Spurred to action, the woman moved from door to door asking for mustard seeds. At the first house, she learnt that the householder's parents had died only that night. In the second house, it was a widow who opened the door. In the third instance, she entered a household where the owner had passed away. Whoever next opened the door, told the woman that his or her household had already been touched by death. As a result, the woman could not gather a single mustard seed from anywhere. The woman then realised the ultimate truth of life, that whosoever is born in this world will eventually die.

This realisation healed her. So she buried her child and returned to the Buddha. The woman told Buddha that he had opened her eyes to the universality of death and begged to be taken in to his monastic order. Buddha readily agreed to oblige which was revolutionary because no other religion in the world was, probably for the next thousand years, willing to accept women as yet in their order.

Another time, Buddha was challenged one day by a Brahmin scholar who insisted doing everything by the Scriptures.

"Why should we embrace your unconventional methods of finding the truth? If the path is not prescribed in the Scriptures, then obviously it is not worth following." So declared the Brahmin priest.

The Buddha smiled and asked the Brahmin to hear a little story. The story was about a charismatic man who had quite a cult following. The cultist had asked his followers to record all his directions in a book. Over the years, the book became filled with all sorts of instructions. Whenever a new problem came up, the followers were taught to refer to that book for solutions. Any other course of action was frowned upon. The followers were advised not to do anything without consulting 'the book'.

One day the leader was crossing a rickety timber bridge, when it suddenly collapsed and the leader fell into the river. Knowing not how to swim, the leader started drowning and cried for help. His followers rushed but as they were taught started searching 'the book' first for answers. The leader kept crying for help but was assured by his followers that they were doing their best to find an answer. The leader drowned as his followers failed to find any advice in 'the book'.

This story made the Brahmin priest realise that one should take the enlightened approach and not blindly follow outdated conservative ideas without using common sense. The Brahmin too then decided to become Buddha's follower.

That was quite an indictment of organised religions which prefer to blindly follow a particular Holy Book or set of instructions. And please remember this was the 6th century BC. The two biggest proselytising religions of Christianity and Islam were nowhere on the scene. But had they been in existence, it was certain that the Buddha would have continued to debate fearlessly with the latter's proponents too about anything and everything.

Buddha kept on wandering from place to place to spread his message of logic and tolerance. After taming Angulimal, Buddha had moved west to the Kingdom of Koshala.

Then having received a lot of affection from the King Prasenjeet and the people of Koshala, the Buddha moved east to the Kingdom of Magadha (the present Patna in Eastern India). The Kingdom of Magadha was ruled by an Emperor named Ajatshatru who had murdered his own father in prison. He had waged numerous wars against neighbouring kingdoms and had succeeded in conquering them one by one.

The local Brahmin priests had become quite hostile to the Buddha's teachings. So they prevailed upon the Emperor of Magadha to assassinate Buddha. But miraculously, Buddha survived all such attempts.

Once the Emperor fell very sick. He asked his Royal Physician about his illness and was told that his disease was not physical but a spiritual one. The Royal Physician said that the Emperor was feeling guilty about murdering his father and for plotting to assassinate Buddha, the enlightened one.

"Your heart is crying for the highest Truth. This is the disease of your spiritual heart. If you really want to be cured, go to Buddha. He is the Divine Physician. Nobody on earth can cure you except the Buddha," said the Royal Physician.

The Emperor decided to attend Buddha's sermons in the nearby monastery. When the Emperor listened to Buddha's message of love, compassion and kindness, he had a change of heart. The Emperor prostrated before the Buddha and asked for his forgiveness.

"I am not your King. You are the Lord and Master of my heart and soul. And I am your unworthy slave," said the Emperor.

"You are not my slave. You are my son, the chosen one. The light of my compassion has destroyed the darkness of your ignorance," said the Buddha.

And in this way, as the legend goes, the mighty Emperor Ajatshatru too became a follower and Royal Patron of the Buddha.

This is how Buddha's following grew from a grand total of five to about a thousand followers by the time he died at the ripe age of 90. Buddha's wife, his only son, his aunt and other family members too joined his order. The movement he had unleashed was unstoppable. His followers kept on spreading Buddha's message with every follower getting ten more followers. Even after Buddha's death, his message didn't die. His followers took Buddha's message of peace and non-violence to not only the whole of India but to millions in Afghanistan, Burma, China, Cambodia, Indonesia, Japan, Korea, Laos, Sri Lanka, Tibet, Thailand, Vietnam and to so many other countries.

Food for thought

What is it that Quiet Leaders can learn from the Buddha?

The Power of one on one conversations.

Introverts sometimes feel uncomfortable speaking in large groups but prefer speaking to people on one on one. This is how the Buddha was able to spread his message. And this is how he gained many followers from all walks of life. Tyrants, hostile priests, dacoits, everyone who came across the Buddha couldn't resist accepting his message. So much so that the Buddha was labelled a magician and charlatan by his enemies whose magic words could change anyone's heart emotionally and spiritually.

And it all happened one by one.

Such is the power of one-on-one conversations.

If you as an introvert are struggling to make an impact, why not start with a few select group of people and let them slowly believe in you and in your vision.

In Buddha's words, there are only two mistakes you can make along the road, not starting, and not going all the way.

"Thousands of candles can be lighted from a single candle, and the life of the candle will not be shortened."

-Buddha

Chapter 3: The Grey Wolf who took on the Religious Clergy and forged a Modern Nation

M was unbearable to quite a few people. So much so that there were assassination attempts galore to eliminate him.

In 1926, a group of men hatched a plot to kill him, but they were soon discovered and arrested. One of the hired assassins was brought in front of M. The assassin did not know who his questioner was. When asked, he admitted that he had indeed accepted a contract to kill M because M was a bad man who was going against his religion and was also harming his country.

"But how," asked an incredulous M, "could you kill a person you had never seen? You might have picked the wrong man." The assassin explained that M was to be pointed out to him before he fired.

M immediately took out his revolver and handed it to the assassin saying: "Well, I am M. Come on, take this revolver and shoot me now."

The man, Lord Kinross writes, looked at him in amazement, then sank to his knees and sobbed.

M was obviously supremely confident that the forces he had unleashed against illogical religious or cultural practices were so unstoppable that even his assassination could have no impact.

But first things first. Who was this foolhardy character M and what exactly was he setting out to achieve?

M was born in 1881 in Greece. He had pale blue eyes and blonde hair. His parents were Muslim but in a somewhat unorthodox move they decided that the boy should be educated in a secular institution than in an Islamic one. The child showed a knack for numbers and was considered as the "perfect one" by his teachers in school.

M's hometown, Salonika (Greek Thessalonica), was a cultural potpourri—a bustling seaport with Greek, Slavic, Turkish and Jewish communities mixing and quarrelling. The city was as eclectic as M's intellectual influences, which are said to include H. G. Wells, Thomas Henry Huxley and Gustave Le Bon.

Not unlike many introverts, M was somewhat unsocial, touchy, and ill-natured that made him quite unpopular. He considered himself superior to the others. But to his credit, M did well in his studies, and also enjoyed teaching the other students.

"He showed also a jealousy, which would grow into a spiteful dislike, of any other boy who was more successful than himself. He would play second fiddle to no one," writes Captain H. S. Armstrong, author of "The Grey Wolf".

At another level, M was quite different from others. He hated violence, blood and gore. He didn't like the cultural practice of animal sacrifice that is prevalent in Islamic traditions and would always try to stop such attempts before any blood could be shed. Once his friend gifted him an oil painting depicting a Turkish soldier stabbing the bloodied chest of a Greek soldier. His immediate reaction was to put the painting back in its packing and have it moved.

M loved flowers and wanted fresh cut flowers on his table every night. He also had a great fondness for dogs and horses. He loved children and adopted a number of boys and girls.

How would such a reserved man, fond of 'effeminate' things like flowers, do in the military, a career that M chose for himself? What would he know about courage, determination and leadership, you might ask?

Well, M turned out to be such an outstanding General that thousands of soldiers were willing to lay down their lives at his command. The reason cited by historians is that M was himself forever ready to die at the battlefield. He always chose to lead by his actions and not merely by shallow words and false promises.

In February 1915, M was ordered by his Sultan to fight off a formidable force of the British and the French in Gallipoli who were bent upon to cut off all sea access to Istanbul. M occupied the high grounds and led from the front repelling the massive assault launched by the Allied forces that had gathered by now the support of thousands of Australians and New Zealander soldiers.

M was a past master at psychological warfare. Knowing that the Allied boys were just surviving on canned rations, he would often throw to their trenches some fresh fruit or tasty titbits that he would have just received from back home. This would irritate and demoralise the Allied no end who in any case were terribly homesick, had no clean water to drink, and were consequently suffering from dysentery and a host of infections.

Still it was not long when M's soldiers ran out of ammunition. Leading by his instinct and not logic, M asked his soldiers to charge the enemy with their bayonets and personally led the bayonet charge. The reaction was so unexpected that it had the Allied forces scurrying down the slopes in sheer panic, thereby saving the day for M and his troops.

The Allies could never win this battle despite losing thousands. M returned to a hero's welcome and was given a well-deserved promotion.

Given his love for flowers and nature, M was once told that it was not possible to grow flowers in the barren region of Ankara in Turkey. The reason, he was told was that Ankara had soil but no water.

"If I bring water to you, would you raise flowers?" asked M.

And so he had a dam built near Ankara and also established a model farm to ensure the cultivation of flowers. Thus M changed the landscape of his country which was once so barren. He was specifically responsible for the "greening" of Ankara, a city that he turned into his capital.

M loved trees and hated to see them cut.

"Find me a new religion.....a religion whose form of worship is to plant trees," M is supposed to have once expressed his desire.

M was determined not only to change the physical landscape of his country but its political and religious contours as well. He hated to see his country being called as 'the sick man of Europe.' He was saddened by the fact that his country was ruled by Medieval Sultans who had no problems allying with the British and the French as long as this could keep them in power. He was outraged that his countrymen were plagued by blind faith and superstition where women could contribute nothing. He wanted his motherland to be transformed into a Modern, Democratic, Liberal and Secular nation state.

It is always easier to speak when you have a cause. Although M was quiet and of a reserved nature in private, he could eloquently speak about his vision in public.

"Our great ideal is to raise our nation to the highest standard of civilisation and prosperity".

This was his passion and he worked hard to gather support for his vision. In 1920 after the defeat of Germany in World War I, the Sultan of Turkey signed a Treaty with Britain, France and Greece (also known as the Allies) whereby the Allies took control over major parts of Turkey and the Sultanate was demobilised. This was done solely to ensure that the Sultan could retain his throne.

M rebelled and openly called for a sovereign state of Turkey. For this, he was soon dismissed from the army. Undeterred, M proceeded to create a National Assembly of 'young Turks' who supported his ideas and called for a Turkish war of independence, a war that lasted for three years. In these three years, the Turkish forces defeated the British, French, Italian, Greek and the Ottoman troops.

With a keen sense of timing, M advanced and retreated. Militarily the Sultan was no match except that the then Muslim world venerated the Sultan as their Caliph or the Supreme religious leader.

M could very well have kept the Sultan in the front and ruled from behind. Instead in an unprecedented move, he decided to abolish the Caliphate itself, and turn the country into a secular state.

The move shook the entire Muslim world. Even in distant India, Mahatma Gandhi was compelled to launch a *Khilafat* movement ostensibly to revive the Caliphate! The underlying aim was, of course, to win over the conservative Muslim and to get them to join Gandhi's campaign against the British rule.

Other nations like Saudi Arabia put a bounty on M's head and called for a jihad against M's blasphemous policies. But those nations were then so weakened by the two World Wars that nothing much could come out of their antipathies towards M.

"Religion! He would tear religion from Turkey as one might tear the throttling ivy away to save a young tree," writes Armstrong. While to the ordinary citizens religion was woven into their very identity, M was driven to separate the very nature of the individual person. Steadily he launched a campaign to change his people's attitudes.

The opinions of M "were the faiths of the People's Party, so that it became fashionable to sneer at religion and unwise and even dangerous to practice it. The men went no more to the mosques. Religion went out of fashion," explains Armstrong. However, this was not all.

M moved like a tornado to initiate a lot of harsh, unpopular and almost unthinkable steps. In 1924, M dismantled *Madarasas*, the religious schools. Next, the Islamic Sharia courts were abolished. The religious brotherhoods and

Islamic clerics were outlawed and almost overnight the whole system of Islamic law was discarded.

Polygamy was abolished and divorce was recognised as a civil action meaning that Muslims could no longer seek easy divorce by uttering the words '*talaq*' or divorce three times. When Saudi Arabia is giving women the right to vote in 2015, we can imagine what M's moves would have done to the cause of women's emancipation 90 years before.

M's goal was to bring his country out of the Middle Ages into modern times. His instrument was the Republican People's Party. His programme was embodied in the party's "Six Arrows": republicanism, nationalism, populism, statism, secularism, and revolution.

From February to June 1926 the Swiss civil code, the Italian penal code, and the German commercial code were all adopted wholesale.

Another revolutionary reform was the immediate replacement of the Arabic by the Latin alphabet. Education benefited from this reform, as modern printing technology could immediately be introduced in Turkey. The youth of Turkey were encouraged to take advantage of new educational opportunities that gave access to the Western scientific and humanistic traditions.

Turks used to have only a single name with no surnames which was quite a source of confusion. So in 1934 M decreed the adoption of surnames or family names. The first consequence of this directive was that the National Assembly gave M his surname as Atatürk or the "Father of the Turks".

Yes, I'm indeed talking of the great Mustafa Kemal Atatürk who changed the whole course of the Turkish and Middle

Eastern history almost single-handedly. If you visit Turkey as a tourist, you will find Atatürk's statue everywhere. He has been referred as a 'Military hero', 'National Liberator', Charismatic Leader', 'Unparalleled Social Reformer' and, of course, as 'Father of the Turkish Nation'.

It was remarkable how Atatürk made Gallipoli, near the historic city of Troy, a place where the Allied forces were defeated so ignominiously, a pilgrimage centre for Australian and New Zealander tourists. He freely allotted land to all countries for commemorating their casualties. When I visited Gallipoli recently, I was awestruck by a huge plaque on Gallipoli's shores quoting Atatürk's soothing, sagacious and very statesmanlike words:

"Those heroes that shed their blood and lost their lives (at Gallipoli battles).. You are now lying in the soil of a friendly country. Therefore rest in peace. There is no difference between the Johnnies and the Mehmets to us where they lie side by side here in this country of ours.. You the mothers who sent their sons from far away countries wipe away your tears. Your sons are now living in our bosom and are in peace. Having lost their lives on this land they have become our sons as well."

Atatürk has also been referred to as 'the Grey Wolf' symbolising courage, strength and agility in pagan Turkish mythology.

Food for thought

Courage, determination and integrity are strengths of character that come from within. A shy person may have difficulty asserting herself but when she sees even a stranger being needlessly bullied or a hapless dog being cruelly beaten, she has no problems standing up for them. Just like Atatürk who was considered silent and reserved in disposition by historians but had no problems speaking up for his fellow countrymen and to see his country transform into a modern, democratic, and secular republic.

Introverts act mostly out of conviction or when they have a cause. Your cause may not be as great as Atatürk's but you must locate one no matter how small it may be. It has also been observed that introverts have their own internal compass and they remain loyal to their internal values. This means that as a quiet person you are very likely to stay faithful to your words making you trustworthy in the eyes of your followers. Just as the Turks believed in Atatürk's ideology and were willing to make any sacrifice to help realise them.

We all have a grey wolf inside us. Our objective should be to find it and unleash its power.

"Victory is for those who can say "Victory is mine". Success is for those who can begin saying "I will succeed" and say "I have succeeded" in the end."

—Mustafa Kemal Ataturk, the First President of the Turkish Republic

Chapter 4: The Courageous Lion

RLM was a shy and a timid girl living quietly in Montgomery, Alabama, USA where in the early 1950s, segregation was openly and brutally practised. Racial discrimination resulting into violence and death was common place. There were notorious white gangs like the Ku Klux Clan who used to hunt and kill black people without any hesitation or remorse. RLM once saw her grandfather standing at the front door of her house with a loaded shotgun because he had just seen some Klan members march down the street and feared that they might attack his family members or burn down their house. This was quite a frightening experience for this little girl.

RLM could attend segregated schools only. Even school buses were available only for white students. The black students used to walk to their schools.

In other city buses, Blacks had to sit towards the back and if the white section filled, the blacks had to move further back. Bus drivers had the "powers of a police officer of the city while in actual charge of any bus for the purposes of carrying out the provisions" of the Montgomery City's Code prescribing segregation.

Bus drivers used to accomplish this by placing a marker roughly in the middle of the bus separating white passengers in the front of the bus and African-American passengers in the back. Blacks had to pay the fare at the front of the bus, like everyone else, but had to then get out and re-board the bus through the back door to take the seats specifically earmarked for them. Sometimes the bus would depart before the black person had an opportunity to enter the bus from the back door!

In case the seats in the front of the bus filled up and more white passengers got on, the bus driver would move back the sign separating black and white passengers and, if necessary, ask black passengers to give up their seats. Every black person, including RLM, knew these rules and had to get used to being treated like second-class citizens.

Nonetheless, RLM joined the "National Association for the Advancement of Colored People" (NAACP) and became actively involved in civil rights issues. She was soon chosen to serve as the youth leader of the Montgomery chapter of the NAACP as well as secretary to NAACP President E.D. Nixon.

On December 1, 1955, after a hard day's work, RLM was simply wanting to get back home as quickly as possible. She was waiting for a bus at the stand, tired and exhausted. When the bus came, she paid the fare and took a back seat. Then as the white section filled, the driver asked four blacks, including her, to vacate their seats.

"Y'all better make it light on yourselves and let me have those seats," demanded the bus driver.

Three blacks complied immediately but RLM kept sitting.

"Why don't you stand up?" the bus driver asked.

"I don't think I should have to stand up," said RLM. She had faced enough discrimination all her life and was suddenly mustering courage to say enough is enough.

"Well, if you don't stand up, I'm going to have to call the police and have you arrested," the bus driver threatened.

"You may do that," said RLM knowing fully what could happen next.

RLM was not being violent or hot-tempered. Yet the police came and arrested her for violation of Chapter 6, Section 11, of the Montgomery City Code. She was taken to police headquarters, where she was later released on bail.

RLM's quiet defiance created quite a buzz in that little town. On the evening of her arrest, the local chapter of NAACP which RLM was involved in, met to think about the next steps. They then formed the Montgomery Improvement Association (MIA), electing Montgomery newcomer Dr. Martin Luther King Jr. as their leader. As a first step, the MIA called for a boycott of the city buses. Blacks were encouraged to stay at home or take a cab to work.

On December 5, 1955, when RLM arrived at the courthouse, she was greeted by a crowd of 500 local supporters. Unimpressed, the court found RLM guilty and fined her $10, plus a court fee of $4. However, the city's buses went, by and large, empty that day. As the boycott continued, dozens of city buses were witnessed sitting idle. As blacks constituted 2/3rd of the commuters, this soon led to a massive financial crisis for the transportation company.

The reaction from the whites was swift and strong. Some churches for blacks were attacked and burnt down. Some houses of the leaders of the Black community, including that of Nixon and Dr. Martin Luther King Jr., were bombed and destroyed. The insurance cover for the cab system that was used by the Blacks to commute was cancelled. Many blacks were arrested for organising the boycott.

This divided the two communities sharply. A black legal team was formed to formally challenge the issue of segregation on public transportation in the local district court. In June 1956, the district court declared racial segregation laws (also known as "Jim Crow laws") unconstitutional. The city of Montgomery appealed against the court's decision, but on November 13, 1956, the U.S. Supreme Court upheld the judgement of the lower court marking a big turning point in the race-history of the USA.

The boycott lasted in all 381 days and became one of the largest and most successful mass movements against racial segregation in US history. With the bus company and the city businesses suffering financial losses and the legal system ruling against them, the city of Montgomery had no choice but to abolish its policy of segregation on public buses. The boycott officially ended thereafter on December 20, 1956.

And imagine, it all started by a diminutive black lady who didn't agree to vacate her seat for a white person. "Her character not only motivated her to make a stand, but allowed her stand to shake the nation."

But first, she needed courage and determination to make her stand. As RML wrote later:

"When that white driver stepped back towards us, when he waved his hand and ordered us up and out of our seats, I felt a determination cover my body like a quilt on a winter night."

The best part of this form of protest was that it was spontaneous, peaceful and non-violent. Such can be the power of Quiet.

You may think that this story is too good to be true. But my friend, the story is based on absolutely real events.

The lady who I have referred to as RLM was **Rosa Louise McCauley Parks** or in short **Rosa Parks**.

Although she later became a symbol of the Civil Rights Movement, Rosa Parks suffered tremendous personal hardship in the months following her arrest. She lost her job and her husband was fired after his boss forbade him to talk about his wife or their legal case.

Unable to find work, the couple eventually left Montgomery and moved to Detroit, Michigan. There, Rosa found other jobs, including working as a secretary and receptionist in the U.S. Representative John Conyer's congressional office.

In 1987, Rosa founded the Rosa and Raymond Parks Institute for Self-Development.

In 1992, Rosa published Rosa Parks: My Story, an autobiography recounting her life in the segregated South. In 1995, she published Quiet Strength.

Rosa Parks received many accolades, including the Spingarn Medal, the NAACP's highest award, and the prestigious Martin Luther King Jr. Award. On September 9, 1996, President Bill Clinton awarded Rosa the Presidential Medal of Freedom. The following year, she was awarded the Congressional Gold Medal, the highest award given by the U.S. legislative branch. In 1999, TIME magazine named Rosa

Parks on its list of "The 20 most influential People of the 20th Century."

On October 24, 2005, at the age of 92, Rosa Parks died in her apartment in Detroit, Michigan. Her death was marked by several memorial services, among them lying in state at the Capitol Rotunda in Washington, D.C., where an estimated 50,000 people viewed her casket. Rosa was interred at Detroit's Woodlawn Cemetery, in the chapel's mausoleum, which was then renamed as the Rosa L. Parks Freedom Chapel.

On February 4, 2013, which would have been Rosa Parks' 100th birthday, a commemorative U.S. Postal Service stamp, called the Rosa Parks Forever stamp was issued. Later that month, President Barack Obama unveiled a statue honouring Parks in the Capitol building and remembered Parks in the words:

"In a single moment, with the simplest of gestures, she helped change America and change the world. . . . And today, she takes her rightful place among those who shaped this nation's course."

Food for thought

Quiet leaders may not pound the table assertively or declare loudly their plans to lead. A simple action like not vacating the seat could be good enough to spark a whole revolution and force your organisation or community to follow you.

And one more thing.

'Quiet fortitude' and 'Radical humility' does not mean that you cannot have the courage of a lion.

"*I have learned over the years that when one's mind is made up, this diminishes fear; knowing what must be done does away with fear.*"

—Rosa Parks

Chapter 5: Was Jesus an introvert?

As a non-Christian, I used to be quite surprised when some of my Christian introvert friends would share their 'feelings' about being discriminated by the Church.

While staying with them for three rather intense years in a Hall of Residence run by a Catholic organisation in London, I had no way then to either believe or disbelieve them. But now after having done some research on the topic, it seems to me that some Churches do appear to prefer extroversion as an ideal and do not seem to be very accommodating towards introverts. What is worse is that they sometimes go to the other extreme and brand a quiet personality as one which 'lacks spirituality' and which 'resists to receive the message of God'.

A person who engages in intense social interaction is seen as being closer to God while those who seek solitude and are drained by socialising events are seen as lacking faith! Possibly from a 'business' point of view, it makes eminent sense to 'recruit' such people who would be super active at the choir, who could get more people to attend the Sunday Mass, who could better garner resources for the Church's upkeep and refurbishment and so on.

Coming from a Hindu-Buddhist culture, however, where meditation and self-reflection (i.e. spending quality time with yourself) is seen as moving closer to God or to the Truth, I am a little surprised. I have always wondered if the Christian belief is somehow related to the popular perception that Jesus was an extrovert.

So let us examine the myth a little closely.

Yes, Jesus did reportedly speak eloquently and did spend time meeting new people and gaining followers, which is admittedly a very "non-introvert" kind of a thing. But from this, can we conclude that since Jesus was the only Son of God, God must be preferring extroversion over introversion?

Before I move on to prove that Jesus was perhaps an introvert, I would like to share some psychiatric research which may be relevant to this topic.

On the Myer-Briggs personality test (which is a psychometric test that classifies people into one of 16 profiles), there is an introvert personality type referred to as 'INFJ'. Let's forget about the more technical aspects but if you google 'INFJ personality type', this is what you will find:

*"People with the INFJ personality type are **intense** and perfectionistic. They have **deep insights** into many aspects of life, and usually have very high standards for their own understanding and accomplishments, as well as those of others. They are **service-oriented** and **empathetic** to other individuals... Usually intelligent and able to concentrate and focus, the INFJ can usually grasp difficult ideas and concepts... They may achieve a level of understanding that makes them appear wise. The INFJ's perfectionism and idealism, when combined with their empathy and genuine concern for others, can cause them to be **true servants** for people in some fashion. "*

Does this sound somewhat like Jesus? Not sure?

Then let's start from the time when Jesus was 12 years old. There is a story in the Bible where Jesus went missing and was found at the temple three days later. What was he doing there?

"...Sitting among the teachers, listening to them and asking them questions." (Luke 2:46).

Note that Jesus was not playing with the other boys of his age and was not scared of being alone. This does not sound very "extrovertish".

In fact, quite like a typical introvert (by the way introverts prefer heavy discussions to small talk), Jesus is seen to be engaging in serious philosophical and theological discussions with adults. This is not small talk that extroverts are generally very fond of.

Jesus was also listening and asking questions, an ability that comes naturally to introverts. So if Jesus was an extrovert, he would most likely be found playing with other boys and chatting away with only a few adults.

Luke's account says, *"All who heard Him were astonished at His understanding and answers"* (verse 47). So, it looks like that Jesus, like any good INFJ, showed a deeper level of understanding that made him look wiser than other boys of his age.

Throughout the Bible, Jesus is portrayed as a 'serious type'. For example, he never laughs! He spends 40 days in the wilderness. Now if you have extrovert friends, you know they will go mad if they are asked to spend 40 days without socialising and meeting people.

Jesus often retreated after being around people. Some have observed that he also quite literally felt the energy (virtue) go out of him when he was touched in a crowd. This could mean that he found crowds to be draining, which is a typically introvert's trait.

Remember INFJs tend to be gentle, caring and compassionate and this describes Jesus perfectly well. Jesus had compassion for the crowds *"because they were harassed and helpless, like sheep without a shepherd"* (Matthew 9:36). *Because of His compassion for them, He healed their diseases* (Matthew 14:14; 20:34), and *because of their hunger, He compassionately created enough food to feed more than 5000* (Matthew 15:32).

INFJs also consider themselves to be true servants of people. Jesus *"did not come to BE served, but to SERVE"* (Mark 10:45). Kindness and selflessness characterised his personality.

Jesus also had a select group of friends. He had only 12 disciples from his many followers. This means that Jesus preferred interacting with a smaller group of loyal friends than with a larger crowd. When he met new people, he only wanted to spread his message and not recharge his batteries in chatty conversations. Socialising had a purpose for Jesus to fulfil his mission. He was not looking to have fun like our dear extroverted colleagues.

INFJs tend to have their own internal compasses that tells them what is right and what is wrong. This internal value system may sometimes be quite different from the moral values that the community as a whole lays down.

For example, in the times of Jesus, a woman who was found committing adultery had to be stoned to death. But Jesus' famous quotation *"If any one of you is without sin, let him be the first to throw a stone at her"* is a perfect example of setting a moral standard that is very different from what the community considers as moral.

Finally, when Jesus is condemned to the Cross, he does not speak anything in his defence but remains silent. This is very unlike his more extroverted disciple Paul who at least seizes the opportunity to preach.

So was Jesus an introvert?

The Bible does not give a very clear-cut verdict and so I leave this answer to you. But there are definitely some very strong clues alluding to Jesus' introversion. Some argue that Jesus was God and therefore he was neither an introvert nor an extrovert. But as everyone knows, Jesus was also a real person.

Interestingly, INFJs tend to be the rarest of the rare personality type. Around 1 percent of the population in this world only is deemed to belong to this category. And if Jesus happened to belong to this personality type, he would be the rarest of the rare, enough to make him unique and God-like.

The short point: there is no need for any Christian introvert to feel that there is something wrong with her.

I hope this chapter has made you feel better if you have previously ever felt that you as a Quiet person were not worthy of God's love.

"Do not let your hearts be troubled. Trust in God; trust also in me."

—Jesus Christ

Food for thought

What can you learn about the quiet leadership of Jesus?

Jesus started with a very select group of followers. Yet Christianity today accounts for nearly 33% of the world's population.

Obviously the followers of Jesus (some more extroverted than others) helped him spread his message around the world.

So isn't it a good idea to influence a select group of people (usually manageable for quiet leaders) and let them spread your influence?

It is also called word-of-mouth marketing by the way!

"And know that I am with you always; yes, to the end of time."

—**Jesus Christ**

Chapter 6: Leading From Behind to Rescue a Pariah Nation

This was coming for quite some time. As the Government let loose its full might against the protesters, Madiba refused to be cowed down. He was relentless in leading a movement against the "lawfully elected Government", which inspired by Gandhi, was non-violent to start with. However, the Government saw a grave threat of violence looming in the background. So they arrested Madiba, convicted him for sedition and for plotting to overthrow the Government and sentenced him to life imprisonment.

In 1962, Madiba was shifted to a nearby Island where he spent 27 years of his life roughly in a small 7 x 9 ft. cell. Every day, he along with the other prisoners was taken to a limestone quarry where he had to use a small hammer to break rocks. The dust at the quarry damaged his lungs and his tear ducts. As a result, Madiba could not cry even when he wished to.

The small cell didn't have a toilet and the prisoners had to use a nearby cave as a bathroom. The guards almost never approached the cave for obvious reasons. So Madiba turned the cave into a great place of learning and exchanging information. Some say it held the most important political meetings of the time.

As years rolled by, Madiba's mother died in 1968 and his eldest son Thembi in 1969. Madiba was not allowed to attend their funerals.

On 12 August 1988, Madiba was diagnosed with tuberculosis. After more than three months in two hospitals he was transferred on 7 December 1988 to a house at Victor Verster Prison where he spent 14 months more in imprisonment. Madiba was finally released on Sunday 11 February 1990. It is believed that Madiba could have been released earlier had he not so stubbornly rejected at least three conditional offers of release.

In 1993, Madiba was awarded the Nobel Peace Prize. In 1994, he was elected as the President of the Government he had tried all his life to overthrow.

Who was this Madiba and what was his story? Let us start from the beginning.

Madiba was born in a small village named Myezo. His parents used to tell him stories about the courage and valour shown by his ancestors. Madiba from his very childhood dreamt of similarly leaving his stamp on the world.

Madiba had a bosom friend in the son of the local tribal chief despite the fact that in quite some ways they were the exact opposites of each other. His friend was extroverted while Madiba was a certified introvert. His companion loved light-hearted banters, whereas Madiba was quite serious and a little boring.

How could Madiba make any contribution to this world when he was not at all as outgoing as his friend?

Madiba was greatly impressed by the tribal king, Jongintaba. He used to observe how Jogintaba used to resolve disputes among men. When Jogintaba held meetings in his court, he would let everyone speak and express their views. Only when they were done, would Jogintaba begin to speak.

"The trick is not to tell people what to do but to form a consensus," Jogintaba used to explain to Madiba. Sometimes it is best not to enter the debate too early. Do not always lead but let yourself be led too.

"It is wise to persuade people to do things and make them think it was their own idea." Jogintaba used to tell Madiba. In the lazy afternoons, when Madiba used to take his cattle for grazing, it suddenly dawned on him that you could indeed lead your cattle only from behind.

As a boarder at Clarkebury Institute, Madiba used to admire the headmaster from afar, but rarely talked to him. In his spare time, Madiba loved being all by himself. Solitude gave him an opportunity to plan, think and prepare.

Madiba was, of course, very sensitive as sensitivity is often a gift with introversion. In school, one of his classmates dropped out. Madiba noticed that his classmate was extraordinarily clever. Yet she could not continue her education because her parents had meagre resources. Madiba realised that it was not the lack of ability that limited Africans, but a lack of opportunity.

At 19, Madiba was already seeing himself destined for a global role.

"I began to sense my identity as an African, not just a Thembu or even a Xhosa. ..... I was beginning to see that my duty was to my people as a whole .... I felt that all the currents in my life were taking me ... towards ... a place where regional and ethnic loyalties gave way to a common purpose".

While working as a law clerk, Madiba slowly started getting involved with the National Congress for Blacks in his country. However, he was too shy to participate.

"I went as an observer, not a participant, for I do not think that I ever spoke. I wanted to understand the issues under discussion, evaluate the arguments, see the calibre of the men involved," said Madiba to himself.

The 1940s were a tough time for blacks. A law mandating racial segregation was promulgated by the ruling party. Racial discrimination had always existed in Madiba's country from the time it was a British colony but this was the first time when a law mandating discrimination was brought in. The draconian legislation classified the population according to four racial groups—"black", "white", "coloured" and "Indian" and accordingly separate residential areas were earmarked.

Blacks were then forcibly removed from their homes and put into segregated neighbourhoods. Nearly 3.5 million blacks were thus uprooted in what is considered as one of the largest and most brutal mass removals in modern history. The government went further and segregated everything. Black children could not attend the same schools as white children. Blacks did not have access to the same medical facilities as the whites. They could not enjoy the same beaches, use the same public transportation and were even debarred from participating in the national Sports teams.

To voice its dissent against such a draconian law, the National Congress for Blacks (of which Madiba was a member) launched a campaign of civil disobedience in association with the Indian Congress. Madiba and 19 others were arrested and sentenced to nine months of hard labour.

Madiba initially had espoused non-violent resistance to racial segregation laws. However, he soon started doubting the efficacy of Gandhi style non-violent protests when the white Government brutally killed 69 unarmed people in 1960.

"There are many people who feel that it is useless and futile for us to continue talking peace and non-violence against a government whose reply is only savage attacks on an unarmed and defenceless people," he declared.

Madiba then helped found a military wing of the National Congress for Blacks. The result was that in 1962 he was arrested on the grounds of sabotage, treason and support for Communism, the punishment for which could even be death. Without a concern for his life, however, Madiba spoke to the white judge:

"I have fought against white domination, and I have fought against black domination. I have cherished the idea of a democratic and free society in which all persons will live together in harmony and with equal opportunities.......It is an ideal for which I hope to live and to see realised. But, my lord, if needs be, it is an ideal for which I am prepared to die."

By the 1990s, the international economic and political scenario had started changing. The Cold War had ended and the US was no longer interested in supporting anti-Communist regimes. The United Nations had imposed many economic sanctions. Riots, protests and demonstrations had put a lot of strain on Madiba's nation which in any case had become an international pariah.

Years passed by. Madiba started becoming a symbol for fight for democracy. The Prime Minister opened secret talks with Madiba. He offered to release Madiba on the condition that he gave up his demands for democracy and equality. But Madiba refused. He wrote a defiant letter:

'I cannot and will not give any undertaking, at a time when I and you, the people, are not free. Your freedom and mine cannot be separated! I will return!'...."

The Prime Minister had to soon resign on the ground that he did not do enough to restore law and order in the country. His successor lifted the ban on the National Congress for Blacks and other liberation parties. The new Prime Minister released political prisoners, and Madiba was also set free in 1990.

"As I walked out the door toward the gate that would lead to my freedom, I knew if I didn't leave my bitterness and hatred behind, I'd still be in prison," wrote Madiba.

Madiba was fighting for a bigger cause. He wanted to build a society where everyone was free and lived in harmony. He had no bitterness in his heart. He was willing to forgive the jailor and the others who had caused him so much suffering. His radiant smile had the energy to discern even enemies.

If by now you have not guessed who Madiba was in the story, let me disclose that he was none other but the legendary Nelson Mandela. Mandela was affectionately called Madiba. His nation was South Africa and the party he worked for was the African National Congress (ANC) which I referred to as the National Congress for Blacks in the narration above. Staunch historians may please forgive me for taking such liberties with the sacred history of the fight against apartheid.

Authorities had banned the publication or dissemination of Mandela's writings. When he was finally released from prison, in February, 1990, most of the world had no idea what he looked like. And that only added to the drama when he was released. As a live BBC broadcast exulted that day:

"And now, Mr Mandela walks through the gates. He's a free man, as of this moment. He's waving his fists in the air, he's smiling. He's a very alert, very imposing-looking figure, slightly greying hair, upright, a beaming Winnie Mandela alongside him."

From prison, Nelson Mandela went straight to Cape Town City Hall, where he addressed a shouting, screaming and delirious crowd of about 50,000 people.

In his 1993 Nobel Peace Prize acceptance speech, Nelson Mandela recalled how like an earlier recipient, Dr. Martin Luther King, he had sought:

"to make a contribution to the just solution ... of the dichotomies of war and peace; violence and non-violence; racism and human dignity; oppression & repression and liberty & human rights."

In 1994, Nelson Mandela made history by being elected as South Africa's first black President. He promised to give himself only one term and true to his promise Nelson Mandela stepped down in 1999 from the post of President. He continued to work with the Nelson Mandela Children's Fund he set up in 1995 and established the Nelson Mandela Foundation and The Mandela Rhodes Foundation.

In 2005, Mandela addressed a crowd in London:

"Never, never and never again shall it be that this beautiful land will again experience the oppression of one by another and suffer the indignity of being the skunk of the world. The sun shall never set on so glorious a human achievement. Let freedom reign, God Bless Africa."

Mandela died at his home in Johannesburg on 5 December 2013. The entire world went in to mourning. People remembered his sacrifices and his commitment. He showed the world what forgiveness looks like. He held no bitterness. He did not seek revenge. He did not seek self-glory.

He was reminisced as a man of quiet dignity, a man with an ever radiant smile and an immense but humble sense of humour. Mandela was hailed as a rare visionary who could see beyond the current struggles of suffering and pain. He had the world convinced that one day the good parts of humanity will trump over its evil parts. Through forgiveness and reconciliation, he even brought out the best in his enemies. He was not a perfect man and yet by acknowledging his flaws, he became even greater.

Food for thought

There is no doubt in anyone's mind that Nelson Mandela was a great leader. But he was also an introvert. In his famous biography, Long Walk to Freedom, Mandela acknowledged the fact that he was an introvert. But was introversion his disability?

Quite the opposite. Many psychologists believe that it was his introversion which made Mandela so great. His biographer, the late Anthony Sampson, thought that Mandela lacked the kind of "political gravitas" early on in his career but didn't realise "quite the steel that lay below." Mandela himself acknowledged the fact that he was not naturally talented but compensated that "shortcoming" with diligence and discipline. This is the strength of quietness. No wonder that introverts like Mandela make the best leaders. Introverts are more perceptive to their shortcomings and tend to compensate by intense preparation and practice.

Mandela was initially too shy to participate in public events when he joined the African National Congress. But far from being a handicap, his shyness and powerful skills of observation actually helped him to understand the broader issues, to evaluate arguments and to judge the calibre of his colleagues. All these traits helped Mandela to become a natural leader.

Introverted leaders like Mandela have been noticed to invest hugely in developing their self-awareness. Mandela was refreshingly humble and forgiving. He did not blame others when he noticed people living in poverty even after he had become the President. His behaviour was strikingly different when compared to the predominant style of leadership which continues to be egocentric, aggressive, self-serving, lacking in empathy and extremely good at blame shifting.

Most importantly, Mandela didn't believe in imposing his own opinions and value judgements on others. As he declared:

"It is better to lead from behind and to put others in front especially when you celebrate victory when nice things occur. You take the front line when there is danger. Then people will appreciate your leadership."

—Nelson Mandela

Chapter 7: The Teacher who stopped Alexander the Great and Knitted a Formidable Empire

In 300 B.C., some two thousand three hundred years ago, a boy was born to a Brahmin family in Pataliputra, the famous capital of the Magadha Empire in Eastern India. Legend is that the boy had the full set of 32 teeth from the time he was born. In awe, the boy was named Vishnugupta, in honour of Lord Vishnu, one of the Trinities in the Hindu Pantheon. It was predicted that the boy will be a mighty king one day.

But in ancient India, brahmins were supposed to teach or conduct religious rites and not rule. Aghast at the blasphemous thought of their Brahmin child ascending the throne, the poor boy's parents are believed to have knocked out a few of his teeth. They then prepared to send him away 2500 miles to distant Takhshashila.

Pataliputra was then ruled by Emperor Dhananada. The emperor was cruel, rapacious and had only one motive to rule: to fill his treasury at any cost. He had taxed everything, hides, wood and even stone! The people in his kingdom were becoming poor and poorer while the emperor was becoming rich and richer.

Vishnugupta's father was a respected teacher-priest and he decided to voice his dissent against the emperor's policies. The emperor did not like that and so had Vishnugupta's father arrested. In prison, the father was brutally tortured and then killed. In Ancient India, killing a Brahmin monk was considered to be the sin of sins and a sure way to go to hell. But even that didn't deter the emperor from brutally executing Vishnugupta's father just to terrorise everyone.

Deeply disturbed, Vishnugupta, as otherwise planned, was sent to the North West Indian city of Takshashila (Taxila in today's Pakistan), where he completed his education and took employment as a teacher. Takshashila was India's renowned University City in 300 B.C. much as Oxford or Cambridge were 1500 years later in Medieval England. Princes from neighbouring territories came to Takshashila to learn the art of warfare and statecraft. Vishnugupta used to teach politics, economics, etc. and was highly regarded as an ideal teacher by his students.

By then, India was facing another serious threat coming from the West. Alexander the Great had defeated the Persians and was eager to invade India. Takshashila was full of refugees who were fleeing from this onslaught. Their tales of killings, burnings and abductions were simply nerve-racking.

One night, Vishnugupta dreamt that his people were reduced to slavery and misery under foreign rule. Deeply disturbed, Vishnugupta pondered on the options that he could have. India was ruled by many small kings and princes, but none of them appeared to be capable of defending India from the invading Greeks. Only a unified India under the command of a Rajrishi or a "strong saintly king" could protect its people and borders from both internal and external threats.

As Vishnugupta recorded:

"Now the time has come to leave the university. The unscrupulous rulers of the country must be uprooted and there is a need to strengthen the country politically and economically. My first and foremost duty is to save the country from foreign invaders....."

The only empire strong enough to take on Alexander the Great was, however, the dynasty that ruled Pataliputra. Dhanananda was the most powerful emperor in India at that time but he was the one who had ordered the brutal murder of Vishnugupta's father. In national interest, however, Vishnugupta decided to move to his home town Pataliputra and to persuade the emperor. He also wanted to meet his mother who he had not seen for years.

The emperor had formed a committee of advisors. The committee comprised of experts, scholars and other influential people of Pataliputra. Since Vishnugupta was an eminent professor from the University of Takshashila, he had no problems being co-opted on the committee.

Vishnugupta was brilliant but could be brutally frank at times. He was also not very handsome, in the classical sense. In fact, unusual for a Brahmin, he was actually quite dark-complexioned and had tanned further by his thousand mile journey from Takshashila. It is said that when this Brahmin scholar met the emperor for the first time, the emperor in his drunken stupor had felt disgusted by looking at his "ugly face". Vishnugupta's acerbic tongue and his supreme confidence in his own analysis of political problems didn't improve matters one bit. As days passed, the rift between Vishnugupta and the emperor grew wider

Vishnugupta, like any classical introvert, couldn't ever bring himself to sing paens in the honour of the emperor. He spoke in extremely honest and blunt terms without making any allowance for any extraneous or emotional considerations. The emperor was not used to such straight talk. In any case, the distant threat of Alexander the Great was not making any sense to him.

So one day he just lost his cool and ordered his soldiers to throw out the Brahmin from his court. Vishnugupta was physically dragged out, with some soldiers catching hold of his braided shikha, the only clump of hair on his shaven head that all monks from India to China and Japan used to sport. When Vishnugupta was thrown out on the dusty ground, the knot of his shikha opened up.

Deeply humiliated, Vishnugupta vowed to take revenge:

"You think there is none to question you? You have removed me from my rightful place and I will dethrone you. And till that happens, I will not braid my shikha," declared Vishnugupta.

For this diminutive Brahmin, however, this task was much bigger than his personal vendetta. It was first a seemingly impossible battle to find the right emperor who could unite the whole of India and defend it from external invaders. A ruler whose happiness lay in the happiness of his people. A King who had a vision and who would not succumb to the temptations of lust, greed, anger, pride, arrogance and over-excitement. An intellectual who learnt every day. A protector who kept his eyes open through his spies. A duty fulfiller who ensured that people observe their duties and who could lead by example. A disciplinarian who kept himself away from bad company and surrounded himself with wise and honest advisors. In other words, the Brahmin priest was looking for a Rajarishi or 'Saintly King'.

Sounded like a Utopian ideal. Would this Brahmin teacher be ever able to find his 'Saintly King'? Would he be able to replace that powerful, but cruel, emperor whose empire stretched for miles and miles across India and who commanded thousands of foot soldiers, cavalry and elephants? Seemed like an impossible task.

Lost in such thoughts, Vishnugupta was wandering on the streets of Pataliputra when he came across a boy who was playing the game of 'King and subjects' with his friends. The boy pretended to be the king while his friends were acting like his subjects. The boy was sitting on a piece of stone, which he declared to be his 'throne'. He was listening to the fictional quarrels of his friends after which he would announce his 'verdict' thus dispensing 'justice'. The boy had a glowing face and was shouting against the corrupt practices of the kings and their ministers. Vishnugupta was instantly impressed with the boy's intellect and wisdom. To him, the boy exhibited most of the qualities of a future 'Saintly King'.

While walking in a hurried manner towards the boy, Vishnugupta stumbled on a sharp blade of grass and cut his foot. Angry and embarrassed, the Brahmin teacher bent down to uproot that offending blade of grass but it was so deeply rooted that it couldn't be taken out.

Vishnugupta sat down, calmed his nerves and tried to think rationally. The boy was watching the Brahmin in amusement from a distance. Vishnugupta took out some sugar from the cloth bag he was carrying, put some water on it and poured the sugar syrup on the grass. Suddenly out of nowhere, an army of ants came out, started nibbling on the sugar syrup and in the process destroyed the grass completely. The boy's curiosity grew till he couldn't restrain himself.

"Respected Brahmin Sir, this was just ordinary grass. Then why did you destroy it so completely?" asked the boy.

"It was evil and hurt me without any reason. All such evil things should be destroyed completely even though they may be small. This is everybody's duty. I would remove even a king if the king were so evil," expounded Vishnugupta.

The boy impressed with the strangely knowledgeable man walked up to him. Vishnugupta asked the boy about him, his family background and what exactly was he worried about.

The boy replied, "Sir, my name is Chandragupta. But why should I bother you with my worries?"

Vishnugupta calmed the boy down and assured him that he could tell him all about his troubles without any hesitation and that he will try to find a way out, if that were possible.

Chandragupta told him that he was born out of a woman named Mura, that his father was brutally murdered by the emperor's soldiers and that he sought revenge. Vishnugupta realised that he and the boy had a common agenda and that both could start working towards the destruction of the same evil emperor.

Vishnugupta was convinced that Chandragupta had all the qualities of becoming a just emperor. However the time was not ripe. The boy had to be first trained in all respects including in the art of warfare and then governance. He needed to become able physically and intellectually. Chandragupta was, however, an eager student and trained for almost seven years till he became a mature soldier as well as an intellectual of some repute.

North Western India continued to face threats from the Greeks. Vishnugupta had spent years studying Alexander's strategies and his vulnerabilities. It was time he put his theories to practice. Soon news spread that two of Alexander's very able commanders were assassinated. It was rumoured that Chandragupta (called Sandrokotus by Greek historians) was instrumental in carrying out these assassinations.

This was followed with a number of mysterious ill-omens such as the sudden burning down of the Greek flag or the desecration of their religious symbols. All this caused much disaffection among Greek soldiers who refused to venture further in India. Disheartened, Alexander decided to go back and ultimately died in Babylon. It is believed that the commanding officers left behind by Alexander to look after the conquered states were either killed or dislodged by Chandragupta one by one. The result was that the Greeks could never rule any territory that lay east of Indus.

Apart from the Greeks, a portion of North Western India was also ruled by a local tyrant by the name of Ambhi. Vishnugupta planned to dislodge Ambhi as he was quite unpopular. He and Chandragupta worked towards bringing everyone together who were unhappy with Ambhi's rule, whether they were peasants, soldiers or neighbouring kingdoms. Soon a massive rebellion was staged and Ambhi was successfully dethroned. Chandragupta took over this region and made this his base for expansion.

With North Western India thus somewhat secured, both Vishnugupta and Chandragupta could devote their energies to the destruction of Dhanananda (the emperor responsible for killing the fathers of both Vishnugupta and Chandragupta). They tried to mount a number of attacks on Pataliputra but failed miserably each time.

Once Vishnugupta came across a mother scolding her child for scalding his fingers because he was trying to eat from the middle of the plate rather than from the cooler edges. It suddenly struck Vishnugupta that he too was making exactly the same mistake. He was attacking the capital directly and not starting from the edge of the empire.

Revising their strategy, Vishnugupta and Chandragupta now worked towards capturing smaller territories of the empire one after the other. After years of war and bloodshed, they were able to successfully dethrone the emperor. Dhanananda was killed in battle and Chandragupta was crowned as the new king. India finally had its 'Saintly King'.

You would have guessed by now who Vishnugupta really was in the story. I am indeed referring to Chanakya, son of Chanak, who has been heralded as a legendary king-maker. He was single-handedly responsible for grooming and guiding the fate of three great kings: Chandragupta Maurya, his son Bindusara, and his grandson Ashoka. In his time, while the capital remained at Pataliputra (modern day Patna in Bihar), the Mauryan empire extended up to Kabul. When a massive Greek army led by one of Alexander's ablest commanders Seleucus Nikaetar dared attack the Mauryans, they were defeated so badly that Seleucus surrendered and married off his daughter Helena to Chandragupta to buy peace. Seleucus also stationed his ambassador Megasthenes in Chandragupta's court whose book Indica is a treasure trove of information of the then-India.

Chanakya wrote some 15 books which compiled together are known as the Arthaśāstra literally meaning a treatise on statecraft, economic policy and military strategy. Roger Boesche describes the Arthaśāstra as "a book of political realism, a book analysing how the political world does work.......a book that frequently discloses to a king what calculating and sometimes brutal measures he must carry out to preserve the state and the common good". Because of its harsh political pragmatism, the Arthaśāstra has often been compared to Machiavelli's The Prince.

Chanakya was also known as Kautilya, the master of intrigue. In Arthaśāstra, he "talks so openly about when using violence is justified? When assassinating an enemy is useful? When killing domestic opponents is wise? How one uses secret agents? When one needs to sacrifice one's own secret agent? How the king can use women and children as spies and even assassins? When a nation should violate a treaty and invade its neighbour? In what cases must a king spy on his own people? How should a king test his ministers, even his own family members, to see if they are worthy of trust? When must a king kill a prince, his own son, who is heir to the throne? How does one protect a king from poison? What precautions must a king take against assassination by one's own wife? When is it appropriate to arrest a troublemaker on suspicion alone? When is torture justified? At some point, every reader wonders: Is there not one question that Chanakya found immoral, too terrible to ask in a book? No, not one. And this is ....why Chanakya was the first great, unrelenting political realist".

Chanakya recommended seven strategies for dealing with neighbouring powers, which are:

Sāma – Appeasement, non-aggression pact

Dāna – Gift, bribery

Bheda – Divide, split, separating opposition

Daṇḍa – Strength, punishment

Māyā – Illusion, deceit

Upekṣā – Ignoring the enemy

Indrajāla – Faking military strength

Can any modern work on diplomacy improve upon these strategies? Can a Quiet person also use these brutally practical suggestions to counter opponents, intriguers, bullies and saboteurs who you come across in every sphere of life?

Chanakya would certainly nod in the affirmative. No wonder, Chanakya's treatise is considered relevant even today!

Modern India has honoured Chanakya's legacy by naming the diplomatic enclave in New Delhi, where all embassies are located, as Chanakyapuri or the city of Chanakya. There is also a prominent road in the area called Kautilya Marg (road).

Food for thought

Do you know that introverts are less reward-sensitive than their extrovert counterparts? This means that introverts are less likely to lead because of power, money or fame but are more likely to act out of conviction, passion or moral duty. It has been observed that introverts are more successful in regulating their feelings or desire. This fits perfectly well with Chanakya's concept of a Saintly King.

A King or a leader must keep his desires under control and must not succumb to lust, anger, greed, pride, arrogance or over-excitement. Keeping your desires under control comes naturally to introverts.

Next, a King or a leader must make an effort to learn every day. Introverts are natural self-learners. Our brain is overjoyed when we are constantly learning something new. We are hard-wired that way.

The only challenge introverts face is to surround themselves with the right people. But introverts also have a highly developed sense of intuition. Like Chanakya who saw a boy once acting out like a king and realising very accurately that the boy had the potential to become an emperor in real life.

Your challenges may or may not be as big as replacing a tyrant commanding thousands of foot soldiers, cavalry and elephants but you must make an effort to learn from your mistakes. Chanakya made quite a few of them while, for example, attacking the core of the empire but he quickly learnt, adjusted and corrected his mistakes.

So as the great Chanakya would recommend, '*Awaken the Saintly King within you*'.

Introverts may be scoffed at for thinking too much and over-analysing but this is exactly what Chanakya encourages you to do. See below what he wrote in the 3rd Century B.C. and how relevant is that advice even today:

*"Before you start some work, always ask yourself three questions - Why am I doing it, what the results might be and will I be successful? Only when you **think deeply** and find satisfactory answers to these questions that you should go ahead."*

—**Chanakya**

Chapter 8: The Quiet Leader who declined to be King

George was a mildly prosperous farmer, of the 1700s, at a time when his nation was ruled by Imperialists. Academically, he couldn't go beyond the elementary school. Yet he displayed an amazing knack for numbers, which landed him the job of a surveyor at the age of 16.

George had lost his father by the time he was 11 but was ably brought up by his mother Mary who was a tough and dedicated woman. For George, his mother was the most beautiful woman in the world. He attributed all his success in life to the moral, intellectual and physical education imparted by his mother.

Since his very childhood, George firmly believed in taking responsibility for his actions. He had a fiery temperament but always kept that checked with remarkable self-control. Whatever tasks George set for himself, he would ensure that he completed them no matter what the obstacles were. He expected the same kind of behaviour from others.

Another strange trait of George's character was that he just couldn't lie! *"It is better to offer no excuse than a bad one,"* George had once declared. He believed that 99% of failures came from people who were in the habit of making excuses.

Like a typical introvert, George enjoyed working in solitude. He once declared that it was better to be alone than in a bad company. He was also painfully modest, so much so that he would say that he was only six ft. in height when he actually towered over 6 ft. 3 and ½ inches!

George loved watching plays which had a profound influence on his character. One such play was regarding the Roman Emperor Cincinnatus who was a farmer in Ancient Rome but was forced to abandon his plough to lead the army against the fierce Aequians, Sabines, and Volscians. After he was able to save Rome, the Roman Senate pleaded that he continue as "Dictator" but he refused and went back to farming.

Another play that deeply affected George was the 'Patriot King', a popular play written by the English writer Bolingbroke, in which the King always had the people's welfare uppermost in his heart. Yet another character who inspired George was Cato from Addison's play "Cato" about a virtuous Roman. George saw the play many times, and even memorised parts of it

As it happened, just like the characters in the plays he watched, George too was compelled to pick up arms and to lead his army as its 'Supreme Commander' to drive the Imperialists out of his country. There was no easy victory. George had to serve the Revolution for nearly eight and a half years without pay. Not only that, sometimes just to keep up morale, George had to pay other soldiers from his own pocket.

George also had to witness the death and maiming of many of his comrades-in-arm, while he continued to suffer additional personal financial losses by not being able to supervise his vast farms for such extended periods of time.

To his countrymen, this proved beyond doubt that not only was George morally incorruptible, but that he had nothing to gain from the Revolution personally. George was just committed to the idea of seeing his country free.

After the colonial powers were defeated, a grateful nation wanted George to become their King. However, just like the Roman Emperor Cincinnatus, George refused to accept that position and went back to farming. This made some say that "he was one of the few in the whole history of the world who was not carried away by power."

George had a vision for what his post-colonial nation should look like. Despite his limited education, he strongly believed that Knowledge was the surest basis of public happiness. He was committed to the idea of liberty too. "If freedom of speech is taken away, then dumb and silent we may be led, like sheep to the slaughter," he said once.

He was also firm that religion will not form the basis of his new nation. He wished for a strong union, a government chosen by his people, a written constitution (unlike the British), the rule of law, an executive with the power to enforce the law and a strong military under a civilian government. Such a nation only could keep his countrymen happy and free long after George was gone.

George's ideas appealed to his countrymen so much that he was called out of retirement to preside over the Convention where the Constitutional provisions had to be debated and ratified. As the delegates argued, George quietly observed. Wearing his old military uniform, George participated very little in debates although everyone knew where his support and influence lay. His role was to act in a nonpartisan fashion and to maintain decorum if things became too heated. In private he argued for a quick ratification of the Constitution.

Despite his reticence, George was still elected to be the first President of the new nation. Earlier, he had refused to be the King, but he couldn't stop people from christening him as the "Father of the Nation". Such was the burden of shaping his new nation's institutions that George felt like a culprit who was going to the place of his execution.

As the first leader of his country, George took steps to ensure that he retained the trust of his countrymen. He scrupulously stayed within the limits of his power as outlined by the Constitution he had got framed. George also sought the advice and consent of the Legislature in making appointments to his office and for executing treaties with foreign governments. He also ensured that he did not make any appointments solely on the basis of that person's social status or friendship with him. Nonetheless, as he was blessed with a keen eye, George could select and appoint people who were best qualified to do the job.

George was viewed as an energetic leader by his people and not simply as a ceremonial figure. He was quite a 'hands on' boss who would ask his subordinates to seek approval from him and who then accepted personal responsibility for their conduct.

George was also committed to the idea of a strong military under the rule of a democratic government. When his officers were angry that they were not paid their dues and planned to overthrow the democratic government, George confronted them by quoting his own example of serving during the Revolution for eight and a half years without pay. Such was his reputation for integrity that George was able to convince his soldiers to accept their submission to a democratic regime. Eyewitness accounts relate that George used his failing eyesight as the example, saying "Gentlemen, you will permit me to don my spectacles, for I have grown not only grey but nearly blind in the service of my country".

By now I am sure you would have guessed who this George was in the above narration.

Yes, I am indeed talking about the great George Washington, Commander-in-Chief of the Continental Army, President of the Constitutional Convention, First President of the United States of America and the 'Father of the Nation'. He served as President only for two terms of four years each and voluntarily retreated to his Mount Vernon farm thereafter. It is amazing that the institutions and precedence he then established, including the two-term limit for US Presidents, continue even two hundred years after his death.

Food for thought

George Washington demonstrated some classic strengths of introverted leaders. It is often said that introverts are motivated more by passion or a cause which they truly believe in than by money or power. When introverted leaders act, they act with a deep sense of commitment and responsibility. Such commitment is exemplified by Washington who fought with his soldiers in the American Revolution without pay for eight and a half years.

Many people also believe that there is no such thing as a 'Quiet Leader'. A leader by definition portrays his beliefs and convictions eloquently to convince others. What people tend to forget is that a quiet person too can create trust by acting out of integrity. Building trust takes time but in the longer run people are more likely to follow a person who promises and delivers rather than a person who very eloquently makes promises but delivers little.

No body doubted Washington's integrity. Even though he spoke less publicly, he was considered "incorruptible" and the best person to lead the United States of America. Yale History Professor Edmund Morgan, in his book, 'The Genius of George Washington', states that Washington was a genius in his understanding and use of power, including when to give up power. This was demonstrated when he had no hesitation in resigning in 1783 as the Commander-in-Chief of the American army and retiring from politics. People recalled how successful military leaders like Julius Caesar in ancient Rome, Oliver Cromwell in England, and Napoleon Bonaparte in France had all found the temptation of political power irresistible. In that backdrop, George's unprecedented relinquishing of power (which he did a second time when he declined a third term as president) was widely heralded. This is, however, quite a common story with many introverts who do lead more by actions than words.

Introverts are often criticised for day dreaming. But a grand vision is also a side-effect of day dreaming. Washington had a grand vision about how his future nation should look like. Dr Glenn A. Phelps, Professor of Political Science at Northern Arizona University, in his excellent book on George Washington wrote that Washington's *"writings reveal a clear, thoughtful, and remarkably coherent vision of what he hoped an American republic would become.*" He firmly believed that a democratic secular government with a strong executive and military would keep his people happy and at peace and he worked hard to implement that dream. He was neither a polished writer nor a spellbinding speaker. He couldn't say much in public meetings, and lacked the charisma of many of his successors. He was not even particularly affectionate. Yet his vision compensated for all these 'character flaws'.

All introverted leaders should realise that they are gifted with the powers of vision and clear-sightedness that others lack. However, to be successful, they have to plan the steps that they need to take to implement that dream and beware of the traps that could stop them from achieving that.

Introverts are very intuitive and gifted with the powers of observation. They use these powers to pick people best suited for the job, just like George Washington who selected Thomas Jefferson, who was pro-French, to be his Secretary of State and Alexander Hamilton, who was pro-British, as his Secretary of the Treasury. Both couldn't see eye to eye on anything and it was Washington who had to give the ruling on any bitterly fought issue. Thus he was skilful in reconciling various views and in that sense he was a supreme politician.

So it didn't matter that Washington was not an intellectual giant in the league of Benjamin Franklin, John Adams, or James Madison. He was the undisputed leader not because of his intellect or ideas but because of his character. It was no surprise, therefore, that Washington had no problems in interacting with brilliant philosophers, thinkers, writers, orators and organisers, such as Mason, Patrick Henry,

Hamilton, Dickinson, the Randolphs and the Lees, almost all of whom were far better educated than he was.

As an introvert, you may like roles and responsibilities to be clearly defined. You are likely to hold others accountable as much as you hold yourself accountable for your own duties and responsibilities. In George Washington's case, this meant drafting the American Constitution.

What is it in your case? Have you thought of laying down roles and responsibilities clearly so that your organisation functions smoothly?

And finally every leader needs time to prove himself. If people have little faith in your introverted leadership, take your time and remain persistent.

"Perseverance and spirit have done wonders in all ages."
— **George Washington (1732–1799)**

"Now, today is the day we honor, of course, the Presidents, ranging from George Washington, who couldn't tell a lie, to George Bush, who couldn't tell the truth, to Bill Clinton, who couldn't tell the difference."

—**Jay Leno**

Chapter 9: The Quiet Mr. Light Who Took on a Superpower and Won

The year was 1910. Vietnam was still a colony of the French.

In quite a common story, the grinding poverty of the country side forced one young Vietnamese boy to leave school, without a diploma. Thin, emaciated, "ivory like" as some described him, the boy first tried his hand at teaching at a private institution in a South Annam fishing town. The venture didn't turn out to his liking.

In those days, it was the ambition of every able bodied Vietnamese to go to Europe in search of better economic opportunities. So the boy joined a trade school in Saigon, sometime in 1911, to learn the duties of a "pastry cook's helper". Such skills about a strange dish had no value in Vietnam, but the same expertise was much in demand by the Europeans of that day.

However, it was some gruelling 10 years later, in 1921 that this young man could manage to sail from Vietnam to assist cooks in the European kitchens. Little did the world know that this quiet frail young Vietnamese will one day challenge History and change the face of his nation.

No one knows the real name of this quiet kid. But the name that he officially adopted meant 'the shedder of light' in Vietnamese. So let's call him Mr. Light.

French were then ruling Vietnam with an iron hand. They exploited hapless peasants in mines and rubber plantations. Malaria, malnutrition and dysentery were rampant, taking toll of thousands of lives.

Mr. Light was saddened to see the plight of his countrymen. On the surface, he appeared to be quiet, gentle, compassionate and fragile. Yet there was a fire within him. Secretly, he had started to nurse a seemingly impossible objective: to see his countrymen free and happy.

Mr. Light's father had once made the mistake of openly criticising the French rule and had lost his job as a result. His family had suffered financially and his father was forced to work as an ordinary labourer on daily wages.

Mr. Light was determined not to repeat that mistake. He was fortunate enough to receive some basic education. And now he had set out to discover a new world.

Mr. Light worked on an Ocean Liner and visited places in Africa, England and the United States before settling down in Paris. Every experience, good, bad or ugly, every interaction with fellow white colleagues made him realise just one thing: that he had a purpose to serve. Mr. Light learnt to his amazement that Vietnam was not the only place in the world that was suffering at the hands of Colonialists. Africa was no different.

When he interacted with his white colleagues, his illusions about white supremacy too came crashing down. To him the sailors and cooks of Brittany, Cornwall, Paris and the Frisian

Islands were as illiterate and superstitious as the most backward of Vietnamese rice farmers.

Mr. Light was an avid reader. He devoured Shakespeare, Tolstoy, Marx and Zola. He was quite fluent in English, Chinese, French, German and Russian. He was most impressed with the United States and loved how America claimed to be safeguarding the rights and freedoms of its citizens. He was also deeply inspired by George Washington, America's First President. At the same time he was disgusted with the barbarities and ugliness of American capitalism, the Ku Klux Klan mobs and the lynching of the blacks.

Given his experience of the French exploitation of the Vietnamese workers, Mr. Light came to the conclusion that *"Capitalism needs cheap labour. The reason why colonised people are exploited is because this keeps the cost of production low! By exploiting foreign workers the capitalist can avoid revolution at home (he can afford to pay his own workers more)! Capitalism is the enemy of all colonised people...."*

This was the time when Mr. Light also became deeply engaged with various associations voicing the opinions of the racially oppressed, colonised and the labour class. He also founded a newspaper which called for an end of French colonialism. He created many revolutionary groups and also took military training. He spent the next 15 years of his life working for a revolution in Vietnam.

Time flew. Twenty years later World War-II broke out. Vietnam was occupied by Japanese troops who committed all kinds of atrocities on the Vietnamese people. Any opposition to the Japanese rule was dealt with public beheadings. Mr.

Light took this as a challenge and an opportunity to create a 10,000 man guerrilla force to fight the Japanese in the jungles.

Mr. Light's actions were noticed worldwide and he was treated as an ally of the United States of America against the Japanese. A few years later, the Japanese surrendered and Mr. Light's guerrilla force took over Hanoi. The puppet Emperor of the Japanese, Bao Dai, abdicated his throne and Mr. Light was asked by the allied forces to form a government.

In 1945, Mr. Light was able to declare the independence of 'the Democratic Republic of Vietnam'. He wanted to model his country on the United States, a nation he deeply admired for its commitment to democracy and freedom. He remembered having read the American Declaration of Independence, but couldn't recall its precise wording. He tried to obtain a copy from the American military mission but to no avail. Finally, he decided to paraphrase the Vietnamese declaration out of his own recollection, declaring:

"All men are created equal; they are endowed by their Creator with certain inalienable Rights; among these are Life, Liberty, and the pursuit of Happiness."

Mr. Light retained his fondness for travel and visited villages regularly. He used to love chatting with school children and sharing his thoughts with them. For him, his people were of utmost importance. He was deeply loved and admired by his people, who often referred to him as "Uncle".

Things were soon going to change. Mr. Light's dreams were brutally shattered when in an unprecedented move, the United States and Britain agreed to let France return and take over Vietnam once again. Mr. Light tried to reach out to the United

States but his appeals were ignored. He even tried to negotiate a peace settlement with the French but failed.

Mr. Light was seething but he didn't lose hope. In his steely quiet manner, he re-gathered his motley group of guerrillas and decided to drive the French forcefully out of his beloved Vietnam.

The task was apparently hopeless. During the seemingly unending guerrilla wars, Mr. Light and his companions had to hide in caves and in mountains to avoid French Patrols. They often went hungry or suffered from Malaria or dysentery. It took seven years when in 1954 in an impossible feat of military strategy, Mr. Light took 40,000 fighters with cannons up the hills that only had jungle tracks and bombarded the French who were revelling in the valley below at Dien Bien Phu. No white colonial power had such an ignominious defeat.

The French surrendered meekly. But their ouster alarmed the Americans who were then seeing a communist under every bed. The United States jumped in, building up a formidable military mission in Saigon. From 1964 onwards, thousands of American troops poured into South Vietnam to divide Vietnam in two parts, to battle the Vietcong led by Mr. Light and to bomb North Vietnam.

America's staunch support for France and colonialism left Mr. Light aghast. To him, America was another name for liberty. A country which had gained independence after leading a revolution against a colonial power was now bizarrely fighting to suppress the independence of another colonised people.

He once told Mr. Ashmore, former editor of the Arkansas Gazette:

"I think I know the American people... and I don't understand how they can support their involvement in this war. **Is the Statue of Liberty standing on her head?**"

Saddened by the fact that America was supporting a wrong cause, Mr. Light still had an unshakeable belief in his ability to attain victory. He once told a French visitor:

"It took us eight years of bitter fighting to defeat you French, and you knew the country and had some old friendships here. Now the South Vietnamese regime is well-armed and helped by the Americans... The Americans are much stronger than the French, though they know us less well. So it perhaps may take 10 years to do it, but our heroic compatriots in the South will defeat them in the end."

The Vietnam War was dragging on to early 1967 but Mr. Light was still confident. He declared:

"We have been fighting for our independence for more than 25 years and of course we cherish peace, but we will never surrender our independence to purchase a peace with the United States or any party. You must know of our resolution. Not even your nuclear weapons would force us to surrender after so long and violent a struggle for the independence of our country."

The Americans were relentless in their bombings. In 1965, they launched Operation Rolling Thunder that bombed North Vietnam non-stop for three years!

Americans put their "Best and the Brightest" to come up with newer and newer strategies. They compulsorily "drafted" their young for this dreadful war which crippled and scarred generations of sensitive Americans for life. Every new weapon they came up with was used on the poor Vietnamese. There were bombs, containing the deadly, and now banned Agent

Orange that would just denude trees to eliminate the forest cover that Mr. Light's boys were using. When there was no place left to hide, Vietnamese made elaborate underground tunnels but kept fighting.

By 1966, war veterans were protesting throughout the USA opposing the Vietnam War. In 1967, Martin Luther King called US "the greatest purveyor of violence in the world," and publicly encouraged draft evasion and a merger between anti-war and civil rights groups.

It was amazing how Mr. Light took help of both the Russians and the Chinese, who were bitter enemies themselves, to fight their common enemy, the Americans. But Mr. Light was getting on his years. At 79, on 2 September 1969, he died from heart failure at his home in Hanoi.

The Americans were till then not fully driven out of Vietnam but the clock was ticking against them. Mr. Light had unleashed forces that were unstoppable. In just four years, in 1973, they drove out the last American troops from Vietnam.

Mr. Light has often been referred to as the George Washington of Vietnam. He was small and frail in appearance with a long ascetic face, a goatee beard, sunken cheeks and luminous eyes. He was vilified a lot in the Western media and people who met him expected him to have a deep seated hatred for Western culture, its people and the American way of life. Interestingly they were mistaken.

An American journalist once described him as "courtly, urbane, (and a) highly sophisticated man with a gentle manner and without personal venom." Apart from Americans, Mr. Light struck a chord with many international leaders.

Jawaharlal Nehru, the then Prime Minister of India described him as "extraordinarily likable and friendly."

A French Orientalist once found him as an "intransigent and incorruptible revolutionary, a la Saint Just." A French naval commander observed the slender Mr. Light for three weeks and concluded that he was an intelligent and charming man who was also a passionate idealist entirely devoted to the cause he espoused.

Most importantly, Mr. Light always had the welfare of his people at his heart. He could be seen wearing his worn Khaki uniform and sandals happily chatting with peasants and delighted children. He was the soul of his people.

If you haven't guessed by now whom I am referring to, the name is Ho Chi Minh, the great leader, revolutionary and architect of modern Vietnam. He remains a legend even now. His people refuse to let go of the memories associated with him, with the result that his embalmed body is currently on display in a mausoleum in Ba Đình Square in Hanoi despite his express directions that he wanted to be cremated.

Food for thought

The name Ho Chi Minh evokes different emotions in different people. Some deeply admire him while others call him a Charlatan. One reason could be that not much is known about his personal life. He changed his name many times and also adopted pseudo names while travelling.

Others criticise him for being a Communist. While it is true that he had Communist leanings but in the early 1920s anyone who had seen the horrors of slavery practised by the then Capitalist regimes had similar romantic notions about Communism. This persisted till the horrors of Stalin's and

Mao's totalitarian rules came to public light. Meanwhile, the Capitalist regimes too "improved" by introducing strong labour laws and minimum wages requirement and no longer resembled the regimes of the 1920s.

However, this book is not intended to support any political ideology. I chose Ho Chi Minh because he came across as a quintessentially introverted person, a very resilient and determined leader who most of the time worked quietly, almost single-handedly, and without any flamboyant rhetoric. It is true that he was supported by Moscow and Beijing but he also disagreed with many of Soviet and Chinese Communist Party politics. Moreover, he always used persuasion as a technique to influence party members and unlike Stalin and Mao, he never used brute force.

That being said, what can introverted persons learn from Ho Chi Minh? He had strong ideals, an unyielding will, a brilliant mind and acted out of conviction, all traits that naturally come to introverts. He was praised for both intelligence and bravery.

Determination is a strength of the inner self and has got nothing to do with being outgoing or extroverted. What I really admire about Ho Chi Minh is his strength of character. Though soft-spoken and seen as a 'sweet guy', he was strong willed and fought tirelessly to see his people free, an idea he always believed in. He was not an idle dreamer, but someone who was capable of taking concrete steps to realise his goals and to make a lasting positive impact.

Challenges didn't scare him. He took on a Superpower and continued even when his odds of succeeding were ridiculously miniscule. He was not scared of time. Whether gaining freedom would take 10 years, 25 years or after his death did not deter him from working towards his goal.

Most importantly he was decisive, and scrupulously honest who never used his tremendous energy and initiative for personal gain. He acted with creativity, imagination, conviction and sensitivity just to create balance.

I think introverted leaders can learn a lot from him.

"Remember, the storm is a good opportunity for the pine and the cypress to show their strength and their stability."

—Ho Chi Minh

Chapter 10: The Quiet Angel of Crimea

When this lovely Victorian lady was just 17 years, she received a marriage proposal from an eminently "suitable" gentleman named Richard Monckton Milnes. In those days, such proposals couldn't be made on the spur of the moment. They had to be vetted and cleared by families on both sides where after the "proposal" would actually be a mere formality.

Imagine the discomfort of the suitor then when the lady rejected the proposal off-hand. The stated reason was that *"while he stimulated her intellectually and romantically, her moral...active nature...requires satisfaction, and that would not find it in this life."*

Who was this person? An idiot or a saint? To answer this, let us travel again, a little back in history.

On May 12, 1820, in Victorian England, an affluent British family was blessed with a girl child. By the time the girl was a little older, she was exasperating everyone by refusing to conform to their concept of what an ideal Victorian woman should be. In those days, as Richard D. Altick states, *"a woman was inferior to a man in all ways except the unique one that counted most [to a man]: her femininity..... Her place was in the home, on a veritable pedestal if one could be afforded, and emphatically not in the world of affairs."*

Consequently, most women in those days only thought of marriage and serving their husbands by learning housewifely skills of cooking, washing, cleaning, and embroidery. An ideal woman was supposed to be idle and ignorant.

However, 'Night' as we will call this little angel, had some other plans. She had a knack for numbers and took to mathematics quite seriously. This shocked and scandalised everyone around her. Unlike her mother who took great pride in socialising with the elite, Night like a typical introvert hated being the centre of attention and tried to avoid senseless gossiping to the extent possible.

Once Night's parents took her and her sister on a grand tour of Europe. While others enjoyed taking in the sights and smells of the historic places around them, Night kept a diary where she recorded detailed notes about population statistics, hospitals and other charitable institutions!

It was not long thereafter when Night reported to have received a "divine calling" to do God's work. She was only 16.

And that calling was to be the menial vocation of nursing!

No wonder, therefore, that in that backdrop Night felt compelled to reject that fine marriage proposal from an eminently suitable young man from a noble family.

Night's decision appalled her parents. In Victorian England, nurses were typically poor, unskilled and often associated with immoral behaviour. The hospitals too had a reputation for being unclean, disorderly and a breeding ground for infections. They were considered more as places to die than places to get well.

Night's parents tried their best to dissuade their beloved daughter to take up such a disgusting profession. However, Night was determined to pursue her "calling", regardless of what her parents or society at large thought about it.

Night started visiting hospitals in Paris, Rome and London. Ultimately her father relented to let her train as a professional nurse in Germany. In August 1853, Night became a superintendent at a women's hospital in Harley Street, London.

The Crimean War broke out that year. The British Empire was at war with Russia and the Ottomans. Thousands of British soldiers were sent to the Black Sea. Thousands were wounded and admitted to Military hospitals. Night received a letter from Sidney Herbert, Secretary of State at War asking her to organise a team of nurses for Crimea. Night rose to the challenge and quickly gathered a team of 38 volunteer nurses from many religious orders. Incidentally, this was the first time women had been allowed to officially serve in the army in any capacity.

When Night and her team of nurses arrived at a military hospital in Scutari near Istanbul in Turkey, they were appalled at what they saw. The hospital was located on top of a sewer that contaminated the water and the building itself. The soldiers were drinking this contaminated water. The floor was an inch thick with faeces. Wounded soldiers were lying in their own excrement on stretchers. The building was infested with rats and all kinds of bugs. Doctors were running short of bandages and soaps as the casualties kept on mounting. More soldiers were dying from cholera than from bullets.

Night immediately set out to work. She obtained hundreds of scrubs and brushes and started cleaning the floors herself, with other nurses and with soldiers who were up to the task. She instituted an "invalid's kitchen" where good food was prepared for patients with special dietary requirements. She established a laundry so that soldiers could have clean linen. Most importantly, she instituted a classroom and a library so that patients could be intellectually stimulated and somewhat diverted from their pain and suffering. As a result of Night's dedicated and selfless service, the hospital's death rate reduced by two-thirds.

Even during night time, when no woman was supposed to stir out of her living quarters, Night would boldly venture out carrying a lamp in her hand attending to one patient after another. The soldiers in sheer gratitude named her as the *"Lady of the Lamp"*.

Does that ring a bell?

Yes, the lady was indeed the legendary Florence Nightingale.

There was naturally a price to be paid for such "foolhardy" behaviour. In Scutari, Florence contracted the "Crimean fever" and never fully recovered. However, she did not allow her fever to tie her down in any way and continued to discharge her duties in as determined and fearless a manner as possible.

Florence wrote about her experiences in Crimea in an 830 page report. According to her, hygiene, sanitation, fresh air, proper lighting, a good diet, warmth, quietness and attentiveness were necessary conditions for hospitals and were to be ensured by trained nurses. Taken for granted today, her common-sense advice helped transform hospitals from death houses, in those days when antibiotics didn't exist, to sanctuaries of care. Her report touched a chord and a Royal Commission for the Health of the Army was established in 1857. Leading statistician William Farr and John Sutherland of the Sanitary Commission helped her analyse vast amounts of complex army data. The truth she uncovered was shocking – 16,000 of the 18,000 deaths were not due to battle wounds but because of preventable diseases, spread by poor sanitation.

Florence returned to England to a hero's welcome. Queen Victoria, the then Queen of England, rewarded her with a purse of $250,000.

Florence used the money to continue her mission of educating nurses in England. With her efforts, the Nightingale Training School at St. Thomas' Hospital was opened in 1860. The education of recruits involved a year of practical instruction in the wards, supplemented with course work, and followed by two years of work experience in the hospital. After graduation, many of the students staffed British hospitals. Others spread the Nightingale education system to other countries.

Florence became a figure of public admiration. Victorian women aspired to be like her. Nursing was no longer seen as a lowly job. Poems, songs and plays were written and dedicated to her. Florence did not like to be in the limelight. Whenever she travelled, she did so under a pseudonym.

Residing in Mayfair, she remained an authority and advocate of health care reform, interviewing politicians and welcoming distinguished visitors. The 'Notes on Hospitals' she published in 1859 quickly became a classic introduction to nursing, and has remained in publication to the present day.

Florence Nightingale wrote about 200 books, pamphlets and reports on hospital, sanitation, and other health-related issues. Though ill and bedridden for much of her later life, Nightingale managed to continue her great work through correspondence.

During the US Civil War, she was frequently consulted on how to manage field hospitals. She was even consulted on public sanitation issues in India for both the military and the civilians, although she had never been to India herself.

In 1908, at the age of 88, she was conferred the Merit of Honour by King Edward.

In August 1910, Florence Nightingale fell ill. She died unexpectedly at 2 pm on August 13, at her home in London. Respecting her last wishes, her relatives turned down a national funeral. The legendary "Lady with the Lamp" was quietly buried in her family's plot at St. Margaret's Church, East Wellow, in Hampshire, England.

Food for thought

Psychologists often claim that introverts act out of conviction and have their own internal moral compasses that tell them what is right and what is wrong. Nothing could prove this better than the example of Florence Nightingale who took up the profession of nursing as a divine calling. She did not care what her parents thought or that the society considered it a disgusting profession that bordered on immorality. She simply listened to her heart. And it was in this way that this quiet, shy, and awkward girl could make such a huge impact on the hospital systems of the world at a time when antibiotics didn't exist.

If you have to succeed as an introverted leader, listen to your heart and disregard the insincere, supercilious advice of others.

If you have ever felt that you are too shy or awkward to lead, see below what Florence Nightingale had to say.

"I attribute my success to this - I never gave or took any excuse."

—**Florence Nightingale**

Chapter 11: A Living god is exiled but the world still bows before him

Tenzin was very disturbed. It was the summer of 1950, in Norbulingka in Tibet, when he suddenly felt the earth beneath his feet begin to move. While people were rushing out of their houses to open places, Tenzin had a sense of foreboding.

This was no simple earthquake: it was an ill omen.

Two days later, Tenzin received a message from the Governor of Kham, that Chinese soldiers had just raided a Tibetan post. Earlier also there were cross-border incursions galore by Chinese Communists, who had stated their intention of liberating Tibet from the hands of "imperialist aggressors".

Tenzin didn't know who exactly the Chinese were referring to. He was after all just 15. He only knew that with an army of just 8,500 officers and men, the Tibetans could be no match for the vicious People's Liberation Army of China.

By late October 1950, news reached Tenzin that an army of 80,000 Chinese soldiers was marching towards Lhasa. Bereft of options, the Tibetan Government decided to consult the Nechung Oracle. The oracle came over to where Tenzin was seated and laid a kata, a white silk scarf, on Tenzin's lap with the words 'thu-la bap', his time has come. On 17 November 1950, Tenzin Gyatso was officially consecrated as the temporal leader of Tibet in a ceremony held at the Norbulingka Palace. The young lad was now the undisputed leader of six million people.

But there was nothing to celebrate. The threat of a full-scale war was looming on the horizon. Tenzin immediately, in consultation with his two Prime Ministers, decided to send delegations abroad to the USA, UK, India and Nepal in the hope of persuading these countries to intervene on Tibet's behalf. Another delegation went to Beijing in the hope of negotiating a withdrawal.

In November itself, Tenzin's eldest brother, badly battered and bruised, arrived in Lhasa. Tenzin recalled:

"As soon as I set eyes on him, I knew that he had suffered greatly. Because Amdo, the province where we were both born, and in which Kumbum is situated, lies so close to China, it had quickly fallen under control of the Communists. He himself was kept virtual prisoner in his monastery. At the same time, the Chinese endeavoured to indoctrinate him in the new Communist way of thinking and tried to subvert him. They had a plan whereby they would set him free to go to Lhasa if he would undertake to persuade me to accept Chinese rule. If I resisted, he was to kill me. They would then reward him."

Worse was yet to come. Tenzin soon received word that all his delegations had more or less been turned back empty handed. It was almost impossible to believe that the British Government was now agreeing that China had some claim over Tibet because Genghis Khan (a Mongolian actually) had once overran Tibet! Tenzin was equally saddened by America's reluctance to help.

Obviously, the two World Wars had weakened the western powers so much that they were in no position to help people with unpronounceable names in a far-off mountainous region in the Himalayas.

"I remember feeling great sorrow when I realised what this really meant: Tibet must expect to face the entire might of Communist China alone."

For the next nine years, Tenzin tried to somehow evade a full-scale military takeover of Tibet by China. He even undertook the risk of visiting China from July 1954 to June 1955 for peace talks and met with Mao Zadong and other Chinese leaders, including Chou Enlai, Zhu Teh and Deng Xiaoping. From November 1956 to March 1957, Tenzin visited India to participate in the 2500th Buddha Jayanti celebrations. There was no hope from anywhere.

On 10 March 1959, General Zhang Chenwu of Communist China extended a seemingly innocent invitation to the Tibetan leader to attend a theatrical show by a Chinese dance troupe. The invitation, however, came attached with an ominous condition: Tenzin could only come with bodyguards who would be unarmed.

An acute anxiety befell the Lhasa population because they knew what this all meant. Soon a crowd of tens of thousands of Tibetans gathered around the Norbulingka Palace, determined to thwart any threat to their young leader's life and preventing Tenzin from going to the Chinese show.

Furious consultations with advisers and oracles followed. The unanimous advice was to leave the country. Or be jailed or killed. With Chinese all-around keeping a hawk's eye on the happenings in Lhasa, the odds in favour of making a successful escape appeared bleak.

A few minutes before ten o'clock on 17 March 1959, Tenzin disguised himself as a common soldier, and slipped past the massive throng of people surrounding his palace. It took three weeks for Tenzin and his entourage to reach the Indian border (on 30 March 1959) from where they were escorted to Bomdila, a town in the Indian state of Arunachal Pradesh. The Indian government under Nehru, the Prime Minister, had very graciously and at considerable risk of annoying China, agreed to provide asylum to Tenzin.

Meanwhile, the Tibetans in Lhasa just lost patience and attacked the Chinese. China crushed the Tibetan uprising with an iron hand. Thousands fled to India to join Tenzin but millions were butchered. Thousands of monasteries were destroyed.

Tenzin had lost everything. Yet in one of his interviews he said "Wherever you are happy, you can call home, and whoever is kind to you is like your parents. I lost my country, but I've been happy and at home in the world at large."

As soon as it was possible, Tenzin met Nehru and started making plans for the preservation of the Tibetan culture and heritage in India. However, his weapon was different. Instead of building an army to counter the Chinese, he chose "Quiet" as his weapon along with "compassion" and "kindness".

Remember, "Quiet" along with its sisters "calmness", "silence", "serene", and "tranquillity" are not weapons for the weak, effeminate and the passive.

Despite the precarious financial condition of the Indian Government, Tenzin was able to persuade Nehru to bear all expenses for setting up schools for the Tibetan children. He then set up a Tibetan Government-in-Exile in Dharamshala (in India's Himachal Pradesh). He established many institutions such as the Tibetan Institute of Performing Arts, the Central Institute of Higher Tibetan Studies, and even a massive Library of Tibetan Works and Archives which houses more than 80,000 manuscripts and resources relating to Tibetan history, politics and culture. In fact, the Tibetan settlements in Mussourie, Dharamshala and in so many other places spread all over India look so authentic that any visitor would feel as if she is transported to the real Tibet.

Tenzin decided to turn the fight for the Tibetan cause into a bigger war. A war against "violent conflicts, destruction of nature, poverty, hunger and so on." The world immediately sat up and took notice. They could now relate to Tenzin's concerns.

Tenzin was awarded the Nobel Peace Prize 1989. His followers were now in almost every country in the world. Hollywood stars like Richard Gere, Harrison Ford, Sharon Stone, and Goldie Hawn were all supporting his cause. Some had even embraced Buddhism. The world is still scared of China but they can no longer ignore the benign presence of Tenzin Gyatso and his quiet voice of reason against the Chinese policies of repression and exploitation in Tibet.

Does the story ring any bells? Yes I am indeed talking of His Holiness, the 14th Dalai Lama.

At this stage, it may be worth our while to go a little more into the background of this quintessential Quiet Leader, simply because it is such a magically quaint story.

The way Tibetans swoon and prostrate before the 14th Dalai Lama, you would think he is royalty but he is NOT. In fact his parents were ordinary peasants who just felt blessed to have a child born to them on the 6th of July 1935.

They also had no idea that the 13th Dalai Lama had died some two years ago and that their son could now be the 14th Dalai Lama incarnate.

There is an elaborate ceremony that is performed to locate the new Dalai Lama. First, someone high in the monastic order gets a 'vision'. This happened when a monk meditating near the waters of the sacred lake near Lhasa envisioned a three-storied monastery with a turquoise and gold roof and a path running up a hill. Next, he saw a small house with strangely shaped guttering. The monk was convinced that his dream pointed to the location of the reincarnation of their future spiritual leader. A search party was then sent to that region by the Tibetan government.

The search party was soon able to locate the three storied monastery with a turquoise roof. They also managed to find the house with that peculiar guttering. The search party did not want to reveal the real purpose of the visit. So they stayed at the monastery and the leader of the search party spent a considerable amount of time observing the youngest member of the family.

Interestingly the two year old Tenzin could immediately recognise the leader and called him out as "Sera lama, Sera lama". Sera was the name of the leader's monastery. Intrigued, the next day the search leader brought with him a number of possessions that belonged to the late 13th Dalai Lama together with several similar items that did not belong to the spiritual leader.

To the amazement of everyone, including the baby's bewildered parents, Tenzin could correctly identify those belongings saying, "It's mine. It's mine." The search party was convinced that they had found the reincarnation of their former spiritual leader. Tenzin was taken to Lhasa and described his separation from his parents as very painful.

At the age of six, Tenzin's education commenced. At 15, he was consecrated as the 14th Dalai Lama. When he was 25, and in exile, he completed his Doctorate of Buddhist Philosophy.

In July 2011, a talk was organised at West Lawn, in Washington D.C. about world peace. Nearly twenty thousand people had come to listen to a seventy six year old balding man who wore rimmed glasses that would be regarded as quite old-fashioned. The man spoke in a very unappealing manner. He took too many pauses. Some of his sentences were in broken English indicating that he was not a native English language speaker. Yet people listened to him with rapt attention. The speaker's face glowed and radiated compassion and kindness. People appeared to be charmed by his mere presence. The man also smiled a lot and waved a lot. People returned his good gesture by waving back at him.

Naturally, this was no ordinary religious preacher. That was the 14th Dalai Lama, relentlessly touring the world and galvanising support for the cause of the Tibetans, without asking anyone in the audience to embrace Buddhism. It was touching to see him doing all this without any rancour or bitterness.

The Dalai Lama's laugh has been described as his most effective weapon. Isabel Hilton wrote in the New Yorker, "It is certainly an agreeable laugh. His shoulders heave, his head goes back, and he rocks in his chair until it passes. It is a great full stop of a laugh, putting an end to further pursuit of a line of inquiry and deflecting impertinence and hostility."

Dalai Lama has been meeting global leaders like the Presidents of the United States, France and Germany, the Prime Ministers of the United Kingdom, Australia and New Zealand, members of European royalty, including Prince Charles and the King of Norway, and civic and religious leaders, including Pope John Paul II and Bishop Desmond Tutu. He has also addressed the United States Congress, the European Parliament and engaged in many inter-faith dialogues and discussions with Western scientists. The challenges were humongous. The Dalai Lama had to speak to people who had no idea about Tibet, Buddhism or his message of peace and non-violence. So the Dalai Lama had to speak in a voice which had a universal appeal.

"No matter what part of the world we come from, we are all basically the same human beings. We all seek happiness and try to avoid suffering. We have basically the same human needs and concerns. All of us human beings want freedom and the right to determine our own destiny as individuals and as peoples. That is human nature..." said the Dalai Lama in his famous Nobel Peace Prize Acceptance Speech.

It is said that the Western mind works differently to the Oriental Mind. Logic, Science, Reason, and even Economics and Business is given more importance than religion and tradition. "Meditation leads to a happy mind" is considered bunkum and quackery but if neurological science proves that "mindfulness meditation strengthens the neurological circuits that calm a part of the brain responsible for fear and anger" then the Western Mind starts accepting the proposition.

The Dalai Lama spoke in the latter language which appealed to the Western mind. He even gave speeches about democracy, business and economics, leadership, environment and feminism, topics that all excite Westerners. This also meant extensive preparation and understanding foreign cultures on his part.

With conviction and persistence, this Quiet Leader even in exile and away from his beloved Lhasa and the Potala Palace, has been able to win the hearts and minds of millions of people. He has still not been able to win the freedom for his people but as the Buddhists say, nothing is permanent in this world.

Food for Thought

It would appear that the Dalai Lama's style of leadership is almost perfect for introverts.

For the Dalai Lama, the most important aspect of leadership is having a peaceful mind. But what a peaceful mind has got to do with leadership, you may wonder.

A peaceful, well-trained mind is important for enhancing the quality of your thoughts and for decreasing your irrational impulses. Negative thoughts such as anger, frustration, lack of self-confidence, greed and jealousy always impair the decision making process.

Calmness comes naturally to introverts. It has also been observed that introverts don't act impulsively. However, day to day work pressures can hamper clear thinking. The Buddhists train their mind by meditation. But introverts can reach a peaceful state by just spending time alone (even if they don't like meditating). In solitude, introverts energise themselves which leads to a calm positive mind.

Introverts are often criticised for taking too much time in coming to a conclusion. We are told that that the world moves on the wings of fast decision making and risk taking. However, the Dalai Lama's style of leadership encourages introverts to take their time in making correct decisions.

In order to lead, you must first understand the reasons for your actions. Then you should be able to critically evaluate the implications of your actions. Do ask if your action benefits everyone or you just alone? Introverts have a naturally analytical mind and this type of thinking may help introverts come up with the right solutions.

If you don't like making grandiose speeches, there is no need to, as the Dalai Lama would readily agree. You may wonder how you can lead quietly if you can't really express yourself. But you don't need to keep calling meetings all the time. Too much formality may in fact hamper communication on a person to person basis.

According to the Dalai Lama, we should practice heart to heart interaction. This means that you should remain approachable. Keep your doors open and let people speak to you on a one-on-one basis. Also encourage your employees, customers, shareholders and well-wishers to share their views with you via email or any other medium which they consider to be less intimidating.

Finally, one should learn the way in which the Dalai Lama prepares himself for any event and how he tries to understand his target audience. He knows, for example, that his Western audience is different from his Tibetan audience. So he deliberately keeps Buddhism out of discussions, even dissuading people from embracing Buddhism. Instead he focusses on business, economics, leadership, management, environment, democracy, feminism or any other topic that appeals to his audience. This has made him win millions of hearts from around the world.

As an introvert, preparation comes to you naturally. Use this strength to understand your target audience and then speak in their language.

There is no need to show aggression or to be bombastic.

Finally if nothing works, be persistent. Persistence comes naturally to introverts. By doing this, any idea no matter how softly it has been communicated can make a big difference.

Lead the Quiet Way.

"If you think you are too small to make a difference, try sleeping with a mosquito."

—Tenzin Gyatso, the 14th Dalai Lama

Chapter 12: Confucius in the 21st Century

Jack Chu was a 20 year old 'International Student' pursuing a degree in Law at the Royal College of London (RCL). Jack was a little upset when he learnt that he, being an 'International Student', was to be charged ten times the tuition fee for studying at RCL than what is paid by native British or even EU students. The posh college, however, claimed in its brochure that they treated all their students equally. Really???

What further exasperated Jack was that there appeared to be no system designed to make life a little easy for the international students. There was hardly any guidance on finding accommodation, opening a bank account, getting an Oyster card for the buses and the London Underground, finding the food that you liked and so on. Even the course work, the assignments and how they were to be graded confounded Jack.

Jack wished there could be a way to get to know your seniors because RCL otherwise was such a huge university that it made you feel lost. Jack thought of requesting for a mentoring programme which could cater specifically to the needs of international students. The idea was to let senior international students volunteer to mentor students who had just joined and put them at ease. This way international students could ask any question about any matter that confused them and the seniors could get an opportunity to make friends with their juniors in a somewhat structured manner.

Jack thought this was a great idea but did not know how to implement it. A ray of hope appeared to emanate from the RCL's Dean of Students who appeared to be a very affable and approachable man. So Jack decided to fix an appointment with the Dean.

The next day at the appointed time Jack rushed to the Dean's office. He knocked at the door and a pleasant voice came from the inside:

"Oh, do come in."

Jack entered. The Dean was dressed in a dark pinstriped suit and a blue tie. He looked to be in his late 50s with greying hair and a weather beaten skin. He wore rimmed glasses which completed his 'professorial' looks.

"How may I help you?" asked the Dean.

"Actually...." Jack took a pause to gather his thoughts, and then blurted:

"We international students face a lot of difficulties in London."

"Really? Then I may be able to help you out," said the Dean.

"That is very kind of you, Sir. The problems are numerous. We have difficulty in finding accommodation or a flat mate with whom we can split the costs of accommodation. London is an unfamiliar place to us. We don't know how to study for our courses or what the education system expects from us. We don't know how to apply for summer jobs or when is the best time to do so. We don't know the various career paths that we can take. Plus we don't get a chance to meet our seniors," Jack was unstoppable.

"That's a pity," the Dean said.

"And this is just the beginning. The list is indeed very long," Jack said and narrated his whole laundry list of woes.

The Dean listened quite patiently and then asked

"So what is your solution, Mr. Chu?"

"Sir actually I was thinking in terms of a mentoring programme where senior international students could meet juniors on a weekly basis. It could be a very casual meeting. My feeling is that the junior international students like us may feel more comfortable sharing our concerns with our seniors than with the academic staff. In this way, we can become friends with our seniors. Seniors too may not mind this because this will not only be a fantastic way to meet juniors but will also be an opportunity for them to include mentoring in their CVs," Jack elaborated.

"Very well, Mr. Chu. But the problem is that such a new programme will require funding and I'll have to prove to the Board of Directors that there is a demand for such a programme. So, Mr. Chu, if you can prove to me that the majority of your colleagues endorse the need for such a programme, I may be able to convince the Board of Directors to fund this project," explained the Dean.

Jack was a little taken aback. He had not thought of these 'complications'.

"Seems like an impossible task," Jack thought to himself.

After remaining quiet for a few moments, Jack asked if he could have a list of e-mail addresses of all international students, both senior and junior from the Dean. The Dean was a little hesitant, because under the strict British laws this could be seen as an invasion of privacy. However, he decided to give away the list to Jack with the stipulation that any correspondence in this regard will have to be made in the name of the Special assistant to the Dean only.

The ball was now in Jack's court. That evening Jack was sitting in the library trying to think about what exactly he could do. Nothing was coming to mind. To pick up something to read, Jack saw a book lying on the table on Confucius. With nothing better to do, Jack picked up the book and started reading.

It was almost 7 pm when Jack returned to his Hall of Residence. He had his dinner quickly and then dog tired crashed into his bed. That night Jack saw something very strange and vivid.

A man came to him with long bushy snow white eyebrows and a flowing white beard. He was dressed in a 5th century B.C robe that Jack sometimes saw monks wearing in popular Kung Fu movies. Then Jack remembered. He looked just like the man Jack had been reading about that evening.

"Are you Confucius, revered master?" Jack asked.

"You cannot open a book without learning something," said the monk.

The monk smiled as if this kind of a response-dressed-as-a-riddle could solve all of Jack's problems.

"Oh God, you really are Confucius!" exclaimed Jack.

Jack was a quiet guy who usually kept his feelings to himself. But tonight he felt like opening up to this divine personality.

"Today I spoke to the Dean about a problem that bothers us students. I also came up with a solution but that was not good enough for the Dean. He wants proof of demand. How can I successfully find proof for him?" asked Jack.

"Success depends upon previous preparation, and without such preparation there is sure to be failure," said Confucius.

"But what if I do fail?" asked Jack.

"Our greatest glory is not in never falling, but in rising every time we fall," declared Confucius.

"I am not even sure where to begin?" queried Jack.

"It does not matter how slowly you go as long as you do not stop," said Confucius.

"May be I should broadcast an e-mail to all international students. Do you think they will listen to me?" asked Jack.

"The will to win, the desire to succeed, the urge to reach your full potential... these are the keys that will unlock the door to personal excellence," explained Confucius.

"But why should they listen to me? I am not sure whether I am the right person to do all of this? I am not persuasive, dominant or outgoing. I lack the skills that my other outgoing, more eloquent peers have," Jack was still doubtful.

"Wisdom, compassion, and courage are the three universally recognised moral qualities of men," said Confucius.

"But I am not so eloquent. I am too quiet. At least this is what my friends say. I need time to reflect," said Jack.

"Silence is a true friend who never betrays," said Confucius.

"What if they don't listen to me?" queried Jack.

"When it is obvious that the goals cannot be reached, don't adjust the goals, adjust the action steps," advised Confucius.

"What if people laugh at my e-mail or consider me mad? Won't that be a terrible mistake?" asked Jack.

"If you make a mistake and do not correct it, that is called a mistake," explained Confucius.

"Am I thinking too much?" asked Jack.

"He who learns but does not think, is lost! He who thinks but does not learn is in great danger," said Confucius.

"I have never done this before. I don't actually have any knowledge about how to run a mentoring programme," Jack mumbled.

"To know what you know and what you do not know, that is true knowledge," declared Confucius.

"Okay but I really don't have any experience regarding this?" Jack emphasised.

"I hear and I forget. I see and I remember. I do and I understand," said Confucius.

"Do you think running a mentoring programme is a good idea?" asked Jack.

"If you think in terms of a year, plant a seed; if in terms of ten years, plant trees; if in terms of 100 years, teach people," said Confucius.

"But how can I make this mentoring programme a success?" persisted Jack.

"...Practice five things under all circumstances... these five are gravity, generosity of soul, sincerity, earnestness, and kindness," said Confucius.

"I am not sure whether I will enjoy such a job. Will it not take too much of my time?" wondered Jack.

"Choose a job you love, and you will never have to work a day in your life," answered Confucius.

"I think I have already got my answers. I should give it a try. I think I should start with shooting an e-mail to everyone. What do you suggest?" asked Jack.

"Wherever you go, go with all your heart," was Confucius' parting advice.

The monk slowly faded away and Jack woke up with a start. It was already daylight.

"What a vivid dream!" Jack thought aloud.

Jack had decided to broadcast an e-mail. So he sat down to write down the first draft.

As words tumbled on the paper in a haphazard manner, Jack reassured himself:

"Thank God it is only an e-mail."

Jack wrote and re-wrote the e-mail.

"This e-mail should catch attention of every international student. It should speak to everyone," Jack thought to himself.

Jack had already done some research on how other universities ran mentoring programmes and had also browsed some discussion forums and Facebook groups for international students. Jack was struck at the similarities in concerns being discussed by international students everywhere. All this research had to be now distilled for the e-mail.

After three drafts, the e-mail now looked somewhat presentable. Jack gave the e-mail a final look and wished himself all the best. He then hit the send button and the e-mail was gone to hundreds of senior and junior international students.

This is what Jack wrote:

"Hey Friend

On behalf of the Dean of Students, I'm approaching you to find out if:

i) You are struggling to find a flat mate for your accommodation;

ii) You suffer from home sickness and wish you could talk to someone about navigating your way through London;

iii) Your professor gave you a B+ and didn't explain what you needed to do to improve that grade;

iv) Nobody is telling you of the career options you have before you graduate out of Uni; etc. etc.

If you think, these are some of the issues you constantly think about, don't worry I am also in the same boat.

My suggestion: *To have a mentoring programme where junior international students get to meet their seniors on a weekly basis and discuss any issue that bothers them. I personally feel more comfortable speaking to my senior college mates than professors. How about you?*

The Problem: *I have already spoken to the Dean. He said that he will need to convince the Board of Directors to fund this project. But he needs me to show that the demand for such a programme actually exist.*

What do I then need to do: Guys I need your help. Let's meet tomorrow in Room 301 opposite the café at sharp 1 p.m. and let me know what you think of this programme.

Senior Students, what's in it for you: *I know you guys have already been through all of this before and had your share of sufferings. But now could be the opportunity to gain some good karma. And need I point out that 'mentoring' will also look good on your CV when you apply for jobs.*

Feel free to reply to this message and do let me know if you would be coming.

Regards,

Jack"

Jack crossed his fingers and hoped for the best. Within hours, he was flooded with replies both from senior and junior students saying that this looked like a wonderful programme and that they will love to meet in Room 301 as scheduled.

Some even wondered as to why the Dean needed to convince the Board of Directors when international students were already paying ten times more than the local students.

Jack was overwhelmed. He didn't expect such a response. His e-mail must have struck a chord. But Jack felt anxious at the same time. Tomorrow he would be the centre of all attention, a feeling he didn't like even one bit.

Jack wasn't very talkative. So he kept thinking of a plan for the next day.

The next afternoon Jack arrived 15 minutes early to feel at ease. It was going to be a big day. Or it could be a total flop. It was now 5 minutes to 1 p.m. and nobody had turned up. Jack was wondering whether he was barking up at the wrong tree.

Maybe he should give others some more time before calling it quits. So Jack decided to wait for another 15 minutes. As the clock stuck the hour, students start trickling in. One at a time. Jack kept smiling. Slowly and steadily the room started filling in. By 1:15 p.m. it was a torrent with the room almost full and bustling with noise.

Jack heaved a sigh of relief and thanked himself for persisting. But now he was going to face another problem. Public Speaking???

With a slight hesitation, Jack introduced himself and then asked others to do the same. After that he briefly introduced the purpose of the meeting and asked "So what is that which bothers you?"

"My professor says that you foreigners write too much and don't come to the point," said one.

"Oh really. That sounds bad," empathised Jack.

"I'm still struggling to find accommodation," complained another.

"I miss my home food. The food here is so bland," was the third refrain.

Jack listened carefully, took notes and let others do most of the talking. Occasionally Jack asked a question or requested someone to come quickly to the point but he let most others continue to share their worries. Students slowly opened up and were able to express their concerns freely.

At the end of the interaction, Jack concluded:

"So don't you guys think it is a good idea to speak to someone about your feelings other than a professor? And in this way we also get to know our seniors."

Every one nodded in agreement. Jack then pulled out a small ballot box.

"If you support this programme, then just grab a piece of paper and write that you so support along with your name and course."

Everyone quickly grabbed a piece of paper and wrote something down. Then they put their pieces of paper inside the box and left wishing Jack good luck.

After everyone was done, Jack counted the "ballots". It was an overwhelming majority who supported the programme.

However there were a few who said that they did not see any real benefits of the programme and thought it to be a complete waste of time.

Overjoyed and excited, Jack took the ballot box to the Dean's office and proved that there was a real demand for the mentoring programme. The Dean was surprised and applauded Jack's initiative.

RCL soon had a robust mentoring programme for international students, which continues even today, years after Jack and his other fellow classmates had graduated.

Jack sometimes wonders what if students hadn't reacted to his e-mail the way they did.

Jack also wondered whether the ghost of Confucius actually spoke to him that night or was it all in his mind.

"If you can't explain it to a six year old, you don't understand it yourself."

— Albert Einstein

While the quotations attributed to Confucius (Latinised from the Chinese name Kung-fu-tzu or Kung-Zi) are found in various source material, all other references to names, characters and places in the above story are fictional.

Confucius, the great Chinese philosopher, composed his thoughts some 2,500 years ago. While Confucius himself didn't write any books, his followers put together a collection of his sayings, known as 'Analects'. These were brought to the West when Matteo Ricci translated these into Latin.

Although very little is known about Confucius' background or life, he was certainly a Quiet Leader. As John Adair in his book, Confucius on Leadership explains

Confucius was a philosopher in the practical, and not academic sense, quite like his contemporary Socrates.

Not many are aware that Confucius was a minister in the local state government, and probably the first person in the world to step back mid-career to devote his life to training others to be leaders. "In that sense, things weren't that different even 2500 years ago. He realised that the standard of future leaders wasn't as required and went about changing that," says Adair.

A reading of Confucius reminds us that virtue, looking out for those around us and taking calculated but decisive action are all essential behaviours that we cannot ever do without.

The beauty of Confucius' aphorisms is that they resonate as much today as when they were first written.

"The man who moves a mountain begins by carrying away small stones."

— **Confucius: The Analects**

The End

I hope the introverted leaders you came across in this book would have strengthened your resolve and given you the courage to pursue your own Quiet journey of leadership. As an introvert, you must realise that you have a veritable fire burning within you.

So what is that fire?

Save the environment or be an animal rights activist?

Inspire others by being a writer?

Work for your ideas without reporting to a boss and be an entrepreneur?

Whatever that quest may be, I hope this book would have made you more confident and motivated enough to pursue your long term goals.

Meanwhile do enjoy the following inspirational quotations from other 'Quiet People':

"In a gentle way, you can shake the world."
Mahatma Gandhi

"Your visions will become clear only when you can look into your own heart. Who looks outside, dreams; who looks inside, awakes."
C.G. Jung

"Knowing yourself is the beginning of all wisdom."
Aristotle

"The beginning is the most important part of the work."
Plato

"Accept everything about yourself–I mean everything, You are you and that is the beginning and the end–no apologies, no regrets."
Clark Moustakas

"You can be a very charismatic introvert."
Olivia Fox Cabane

"In order to carry a positive action we must develop here a positive vision."
Dalai Lama

"Give me six hours to chop down a tree and I will spend the first four sharpening the axe."
Abraham Lincoln

"Wise men speak because they have something to say; Fools because they have to say something."
Plato

"Be faithful in small things because it is in them that your strength lies."
Mother Teresa

Books by Prasenjeet Kumar in the Quiet Phoenix Series

CELEBRATING QUIET PEOPLE: UPLIFTING STORIES FOR INTROVERTS AND HIGHLY SENSITIVE PERSONS

QUIET PHOENIX: AN INTROVERT'S GUIDE TO RISING IN CAREER & LIFE

QUIET PHOENIX 2: FROM FAILURE TO FULFILMENT: A MEMOIR OF AN INTROVERTED CHILD

CELEBRATING QUIET LEADERS: UPLIFTING STORIES OF INTROVERTED LEADERS WHO CHANGED HISTORY

CELEBRATING QUIET ARTISTS: STIRRING STORIES OF INTROVERTED ARTISTS THE WORLD CAN'T FORGET

FICTION by Prasenjeet Kumar

THE MURDER OF MR. SACHDEVA

THE FORBIDDEN TRUTH: SEASON ONE

THE FORBIDDEN TRUTH: SEASON TWO

THE FORBIDDEN TRUTH: SEASON FINALE

LEGALLY IN LOVE

LOVE KARMA CROSSED

WHEN GANGES MET THE NORTH SEA

YOU CAN'T KILL MY LOVE: A KASHMIR HOLOCAUST LOVE STORY

AUTISTICALLY YOURS

STILL MISSING...

WHEN YOU CAN'T TRUST LOVE

THE ENEMY WITHIN

THE SCEPTIC

FICTION by Arun Kumar and Prasenjeet Kumar

KASHMIR IS FREE

KASHMIR THINKS ITS FREE

KASHMIR IS FREE FINALLY

Books by Prasenjeet Kumar in the "Self-Publishing WITHOUT SPENDING A DIME" Series

HOW TO BE AN AUTHOR ENTREPRENEUR WITHOUT SPENDING A DIME

HOW TO TRANSLATE YOUR BOOKS WITHOUT SPENDING A DIME

HOW TO MARKET YOUR BOOKS WITHOUT SPENDING A DIME

HOW TO HAVE A HAPPIER WRITER MINDSET WITHOUT SPENDING A DIME

Cookbooks by Prasenjeet Kumar (with Sonali Kumar)

HOME STYLE INDIAN COOKING IN A JIFFY

HOW TO COOK IN A JIFFY EVEN IF YOU HAVE NEVER BOILED AN EGG BEFORE

HEALTHY COOKING IN A JIFFY: THE COMPLETE NO FAD NO DIET HANDBOOK

HOW TO CREATE A COMPLETE MEAL IN A JIFFY

THE ULTIMATE GUIDE TO COOKING LENTILS THE INDIAN WAY

THE ULTIMATE GUIDE TO COOKING RICE THE INDIAN WAY

THE ULTIMATE GUIDE TO COOKING FISH THE INDIAN WAY

THE ULTIMATE GUIDE TO COOKING CHICKEN THE INDIAN WAY

THE ULTIMATE GUIDE TO COOKING VEGETABLES THE INDIAN WAY

THE ULTIMATE GUIDE TO COOKING DESSERTS THE INDIAN WAY

THE ULTIMATE INDIAN INSTANT POT COOKBOOK

Acknowledgment

To my dear mother and father for their unflinching support and belief in my abilities without which I couldn't have written this book.

Disclaimer

This book is not intended to hurt any one's religious sentiments or political, racial or national views or to be used for proselytising.

Connect With The Author

Please do feel free to visit us at: http://publishwithprasen.com

Should you have any questions or comments, please do not hesitate to write to us anytime at: prasenjeet@publishwithprasen.com OR prasenpublishers@gmail.com.

We would also love to connect with you on social media.

Join us on:

Twitter

https://twitter.com/publishwithprasen

Goodreads

https://www.goodreads.com/prasenjeet

About The Author

Prasenjeet Kumar is the author/co-author of over 39 books in four genres: Fiction, motivational books for introverts (the Quiet Phoenix series), books on Self-Publishing (Self-Publishing WITHOUT SPENDING A DIME series) and cookbooks (Cooking In A Jiffy series). His books (over 100 titles and counting) have been translated into French, German, Italian, Japanese, Spanish, and Portuguese, and sell in over 50 countries.

Prasenjeet is a Law graduate from the University College London (2005-2008), London University and a Philosophy Honours graduate from St. Stephen's College (2002-2005), Delhi University. In addition, he holds a Legal Practice Course (LPC) Diploma from College of Law, Bloomsbury, London, and was for a brief while, a solicitor of England and Wales.

Prasenjeet loves gourmet food, music, films, and travelling. He has already covered thirty-six countries including Australia, Canada, China, Denmark, Dubai, Egypt, Estonia, Finland, France, Germany, Greece, Hong Kong, Iceland, Indonesia, Israel, Italy, Jordan, Latvia, Lithuania, Macau, Malaysia, Mauritius, Monaco, Montenegro, Nepal, New Zealand, Norway, Sharjah, Spain, Sweden, Switzerland, Thailand, Turkey, UK, Uzbekistan, and the USA.

Prasenjeet is the self-taught designer, writer, editor, and proud owner of the website cookinginajiffy.com which he has dedicated to his mother. He also runs another website publishwithprasen.com where he shares tips about writing and self-publishing.